As Figs in Autumn

As Figs in Autumn

One Year in a Forever War

A Memoir

Ben Bastomski

DELPHINIUM BOOKS

AS FIGS IN AUTUMN

No part of this book may be used or reproduced in any manner whatsoever without written permission of the publisher except in the case of brief quotations embodied in critical articles and reviews.
For information, address DELPHINIUM BOOKS, INC., 16350 Ventura Boulevard, Suite D
PO Box 803
Encino, CA 91436

Library of Congress Cataloguing-in-Publication Data is available on request.
ISBN 978-1-953002-24-2

23 24 25 26 27 LBC 5 4 3 2 1

Jacket and interior design by Colin Dockrill, AIGA

Acknowledgment is made for permission to reprint "A Man in His Life" from *The Poetry of Yehuda Amichai* (2015)by Yehuda Amichai, edited by Robert Alter. Translated by Chana Bloch. Reprinted by the permission of the Yehuda Amichai Estate in cooperation with The Deborah Harris Agency.

FOR DOTAN

PART I

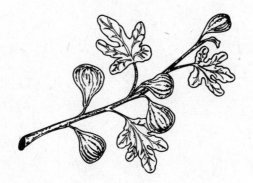

1.

As a rule, the dogs were quiet. They liked to guard in pairs, so that each had less reason to break from silence than if he were alone, and together they would sit, and look to the west beyond the barbed wire.

If they broke the silence, it was for a reason, which was nearly all that could be asked of a guard dog. But even if they were better than human in this regard, they were not immune, and often barked when the birds soared low in the sky above, no threat to anyone but the dogs in the narrow corridor between two tall rows of wire at the edge of the grounds. Once the birds flew off, they returned to their routine as if they had never been disturbed, as if there were no second fence behind them at all.

I sat on the hill inside both fences and ate oranges from the field below, the sun dipping in the west and light dancing in the trees, an enchanted image but one the dogs never looked behind to see. Barking now, one then the other. I brought my eyes to the two of them tensed on their feet, and searched up above but found empty air. Two dogs howling at a fading sky with no birds. Then came the first call.

Tzeva Adom.

I had fifteen seconds, and there was a shelter near the field on the map they had given me my first day but I could not recall where. Instead I grabbed for my rifle, it would protect me from the rockets falling, it was not here, it was safe in my room at the far end of the grounds, safe, a place I was not. And I searched but saw no shelter, just the locked shed and the tractor and the light dancing in the orange trees, and the dogs at the fence beyond.

Tzeva Adom.

The dogs were frenzied but her call was calm. Eleven seconds and no shelter, only the open field. Here was as good as the next spot, as though arriving at a vast and pristine shore and choosing where, in the endless white sand, to lie down awhile. Here. Remembering what I was taught, I lay facedown, arms over head in protection, body prone on the earth, in submission. My urge was to curl, like a fetus, but it was wrong, would make me taller when what saved was lowness, closeness to the soil. The dirt, the cracks, the lone ant running in the fissures of the earth.

Tzeva Adom.

Her third call came calmest yet. The others near the shelters had seven seconds to reach them, hearts pounding, stampeding on the earth. Yet here lying in the field, I had completed preparations, freed of any further cause for struggle, for alarm. A gift of seven seconds.

So they slowed. The savage barking of the dogs, the screams piercing the air came from far, faint, foreign, the cotton texture of a dream. My language was the mighty ant speeding in the cracks of the earth, six armored black legs in perfected rhythm. He was unbreakable, he was ageless. He left nothing.

Tzeva Adom.

The explosions, too, came from far. With the last I pulled my lips from the dirt and watched the tiny ant wriggle from the crack into which he had fallen, and join the long column of others I had not seen in lying prone. I sat upright, and the light struck the swaying orange trees at an angle more entrancing than before. Autumn was not yet their fullest season, but already many bore fruit that fell from the branches to the earth, to set the table for the great tribes of ants, and the spoils for their wars.

The light was leaving now, and I picked up the sweet orange I had dropped in the alarm and, as I ate, watched the dogs, who had gone quiet as after the retreat of a low-flying bird. There, now, a pair of doves climbing the firmament, awash in the late golden light—but the guards were unmoved, gazing west. It was not that they did not see the doves, but that at such great height, they were no threat to anyone at all.

2.

I have set watchmen on your walls, O Jerusalem,
Who shall never hold their peace day nor night.
—Isaiah, 62:6

An atheist, after all, is only an agnostic who has decided to make it personal. An agnostic with a grudge. This is what I told myself, anyway, as I put hand over hand on the oxidized ladder and climbed these last few green rungs toward the kingdom of heaven. I took up my position alone in this darkened watchtower and withdrew my arms to within my uniform for warmth, wrapping them around my chest instead of my M4A1 carbine, which hung from my neck by its leather strap, flaccid as my two empty sleeves beside it. Jerusalem's guardian. There may be no atheist in a foxhole, but surely one might be found shivering in a sand-blasted turret alone in the Negev.

And the morning light came warm in our army tent, always warmest after a night in the tower before. My cot was fifth on the left, a lucky in-between of darkness and light, close enough to the heavy tent flaps to catch a sunbeam when they were thrown open at dawn, far enough to be untroubled by the lampposts shining through the cracks at night. Now came the sunbeam and the commander's call, the grinding zippers of our sleeping bags, wriggling in two rows from our green cocoons and discarding them, as though we expected not to regress into them again.

This morning we tossed them with recklessness, because

it was Friday and tonight we slept elsewhere, would not crawl back into these till Sunday, and that Sunday might someday come was no future to believe in. We rose to dress in our proud *aleph* instead of *bet*, to salute our flag together and be on our way home, because although we were not yet qualified for our secondary function of fighting for the land, we had long begun our first of wearing her colors. Since it was critical to keep these two functions apart, one was given a separate costume for each one. The primary costume, of course, took the alphabet's first letter, *aleph*, and it was regal, a stiff weave that made your limbs look square and hard beneath. Its fabric was bulletproof, because everyone knew this was not a costume one could be killed in, since that function was reserved for the alphabet's inferior letter, *bet*. This secondary costume was filthy straight out of the wash, a thicker fabric that was nonetheless highly penetrable, gripped the skin it sat on, like the earth one stood on. There had been no monuments built to *bet* despite its sacrifices, and *bet* was fine with that. And though we had come with *aleph* in our eyes, it seemed there was more to learn from *bet*, which I imagined was why they had us wear it nearly all the time.

Bet had a hole in each armpit, so that if you took a sniper's round or a knife or a spiraling slice of shrapnel to the chest and the medics had to cut away your shirt to treat your wounds, they would have a head start. *Aleph* had no gaps in its fabric and never understood why *bet* had such a horrid imagination, and nor did we, when it came time to wear our primaries again. So we donned *aleph* and the tent filled with the scent of body spray antiperspirant, which was the scent of *aleph*, and we tucked in our shirts as only *aleph* was finicky about, and assembled on the yard. We stood to salute the flag and I watched it fly above, but also my men around, because to see them stand in *aleph* made me swell, and reminded me why I had come. Then we were dismissed, and we were on the army bus to the nearby transit station to begin our way home.

We disembarked at the station and each soldier was off to find his bus—but I was in no rush for mine and not prepared to fight like I would need to if I wanted the first one. So as the bus pulled in, I kept a distance as it stirred a wave through the waiting throng, each of the men locking his stance and shoving about him to win passage home. A band of us kept planted on the curbs and walls in tired amusement as the others fought, an ironic melee amid the automatic rifles that hung from their backs, swinging in hard clacks against one another while the soft bodies scuffled in green. The bus kept filling till armed to the teeth, green shirts all along the aisle and black rifle tips poking at the windows. Finally its doors sealed, shutting out the last contestants, who joined us where we sat and watched the bus roll out, apocalyptically armed, to the road ahead.

There were at least another twenty minutes till the next bus, though if it ended up an hour, that, too, would be fine. The treasured part of home was not in the house's warm food and linens but in the air beyond the walls of the base. It was in being unbeholden to any clock, free in each motion and thought, a home that began here at the station and not the house. To forsake this home and throw myself into combat for a seat—now, when at last no combat was asked of me—would be senseless, inhuman. And so I moved not a muscle, intent only on this space between.

I had nothing to say to the men sitting to my left and right, whose black and turquoise berets said they were in Armored and Artillery, respectively. Armored sat back with headphones while his rifle barrel rested across my lap, which was fine, and Artillery ate Bamba peanut butter puffs from a plastic bag, rubbing his fingers between grabs and dusting my lap and Armored's rifle, which was fine with me and him, too. No one said much, and none of us had much to say about that, and in feeling the same way about that, there was great closeness, which we also agreed was better than trying to talk to find closeness instead.

The other two wore sunglasses, a nice completing touch on *aleph* but one I went without, because such reverent shades on the eyes can blind them to the helpful truth that the sun, too, is often forced into hiding. It was smothered now by the clouds, the fount of all earthly might snuffed out by soft white morning sheets. And though it seemed to make little difference to the others behind their heavy black lenses, I saw, and I stared into it for now, while I could.

The sun was still hiding when the barrel came off my thigh and Armored rose to his feet. We were few enough to fit on the new bus without altercation, placid as we filtered on. I flipped my ID to the driver, found an aisle seat several rows back, and sat, resting my rifle in my lap and my head on the seat's hard leather back. Then I went to dim, a higher bliss than sleep. Nearly all the lights off, save for a happy few neurons staying up late to savor the feeling. My head, somewhere far, nodded and drifted to the center of the aisle. Then came the scent of a woman.

In the aisle ahead stood a soldier, black hair and black rifle resting at her back. She wore *aleph*, which made her look square and hard beneath, making one ache to think what she might look like in *bet*. She was doused in perfume that conjured vanilla and bourbon, things forbidden both by rule and by default in the desert I inhabited. She started toward me, a vision gliding between limp necks and buzzed heads in the aisle, twisting her shoulders to make her way. Then her long black hair had whirled onto my face slumped in the aisle, clung to my cheeks, and tugged across my skin. Her rifle had to have been slung across the far side of her back or I might have had its barrel to my face instead, which would have been gentler of her. Her hair was barbarically soft and, unlike her barrel, was a thing I had lost all acquaintance with.

She paused on her way past, slowing her hair's friction along my prone forehead, and I swallowed, spine rigid, hands finding their way to my rifle. Then she was gone, had found a seat farther down the aisle, leaving me wide awake with one black vanilla-bourbon strand that had chosen to stay. This was one strand too many, so I plucked it off my forehead, though its scent would stay awhile. I closed my eyes again and drifted back under, eyes flitting, lips slacked, seeing one more fleeting vision of the brown-eyed recruit in the back of the bus, before more familiar and comforting visions of nothing at all.

3.

Israel is my middle name. In Hebrew, it is my first: Yisrael. Long before it came to be the name of any state, this was the earned name of Jacob, he who wrestled with God (*Yisrael*: "wrestles with God"). Then, it was the name of the patrilineal Hebrew caste into which I was born. Having neither the ascended station of Levite nor of Kohen, a Yisrael was a rank-and-file commoner, right at home where the undistinguished rows of recruits slept on stiff leather seats.

This cradle's rigid, military-grade black leather had a way of governing the texture even of my half remembrances and dreams. It imprinted a certain hard, orderly affection, giving precious little room for dalliances and make-believe, and the truth was that I had never intended to be a soldier and not one here, where before this I had spent just a few weeks in tour buses with plusher seats, had not known the language nor a soul before being dropped at Ben Gurion in the fall and boot camp a month later. Yet now, I was one, a state of affairs that most astonished not in the thralls of training but in these lengths of breathing room between.

Even this freedom, too, was military-grade, drawn and structured, bounded strictly by the authority that formed it, shaped it, and towered on all its four sides, a freedom stamped in triplicate with the seal of the machine. My aching bones on this unforgiving leather, I had been rationed not even the whim to dream it all away, let alone the means. Rather, in this breathing room confronted with my soldierhood all the more, I was brought not to escape it but unearth it. Because I had jumped aboard this bus with little forethought, I did most of my appraising after the fact: examining the long unbroken chain that finished on a bus where I had every reason to be.

Before it came to be the name of any state, Yisrael was, too, the name of my father's father's father, for whom I was named. I never met him, which was in accord with the rule: Ashkenazi Jews do not name children after living relatives, only in remembrance of the dead—therefore, a remembrance not really mine, but quite alive in Yisrael Bastomski's son, Yitzchak Bastomski. My *zayde* Yitzchak survived the Warsaw Ghetto, and met my *bubbe*, an Auschwitz survivor, in a displaced persons camp after the war. He knew at once what he had found, and after a courtship unmarked by much of any pretense, he committed to a lifetime of surviving with her, which is to say (and contrary to inconversant Hallmark notions), to a *higher* form of living, and one they would pursue each day.

They came together to America and chose the Jewish frontier of Los Angeles, where he ran a thriving glatt kosher butcher shop, and they raised ten children in a home they gave to honoring and embodying their faith. Not just living, but surviving, the latter not a call to mere subsistence, but intactness. (Before the English lost it in translation, the French had this right: *vivre* is "to live," and the prefix *sur-* in *survivre*, "to survive," expresses "over" or "super," to lend the basic verb a higher strength.) My father was the third child and second son, and I was not the firstborn grandchild: my father's older sister had sons first, and his older brother had daughters. I was, however, among the dozens in my generation, the first son born to a son of my grandparents: the eldest grandchild born with the Bastomski name who, by custom, for all his life would keep it. For this, I was called Yisrael Bastomski, a name reserved for me—or rather, for the first one born to take it.

My *zayde* would call me this, Yisrael, his father's name and mine, or mouth it to me in the way I treasured. By the time

I was old enough to remember, he had developed Parkinson's disease, which forced him from his profession, gave him a tremble, and came to take the vigor from his words. But on the wall of his living room, above the chair where he would rest, was my favorite black-and-white portrait of him as a younger man, handsome and broad-shouldered, a felt cap tilted on his brow and his eyes resting firmly forward, to where I stood before him. I watched this image when he sat beneath it and spoke to me, and though his words did not reach my ears, I could hear them in the voice of the man who looked back at me above, and I listened as the two of them spoke, until he was done, and he was telling me he loved me, and I told him I loved him, too.

"Take me with you." This is what my *bubbe* cried aloud, over and over, as they lowered him to his grave.

When my *zayde* died in my second year of college, the grief it threw me to was not so sharp and wrenching—my *zayde*, after all, had kept surviving well into his nineties—but more liturgical and sober, less a cutting trauma than a stern calling to account. Yisrael, the name he called me, had always been both an honor and a charge, yet never until now had the second felt so conscious, nor so unnamed.

It happened that I was deepening my study in ethics and political philosophy, the degree to which I had committed earlier that year. My favorite then was Arendt, perhaps the most unmerciful restructurer to the frame of reference I had brought to college. "For legends," she wrote in *The Origins of Totalitarianism*, "attract the very best in our times, just as ideologies attract the average, and the whispered tales of gruesome secret powers behind the scenes attract the very worst." This, I thought, was an exquisite framing. One I read, reread, and bookmarked the first time I encountered it, one I returned to on the passing of my *zayde*, pursuer of a legend, and last rememberer of the other Yisrael than me.

4.

In truth, the extent to which it felt as though this were the wrong bus was merely the extent to which I had not done the needed excavation. I did not pretend to have done all or even most of it before boarding, which was why it now came as such a recurring theme. And there were many pieces to the unbroken chain that finished on this bus, many *reasons* this was not the wrong one, but they were not the *cause* that brought me to it. Reasons may grow apparent only in the full glow of hindsight, long after causes hit us in the dark across the face.

I was pulled awake now at a changing of the guard at the window seat beside me, and another soldier squeezing in to take the seat. Paratroopers, said his maroon beret. This kind of internal interruption was what it took to rouse me, because otherwise our bus's mighty shock absorbers kept one sheltered like a spell even from the craggiest of jolts on the highway. Paratroopers carried the distinctive scent of body spray antiperspirant, which was the scent of *aleph*, to which by nature I had no objection. (Vanilla and bourbon were now beyond all recollection.) As he settled and closed his eyes, his rifle barrel came to sit across my thigh, which was fine, and as his head rested on my shoulder, this was fine, too. He had not said a word beforehand, which would have been an odd and stuffy thing to do, and as was the case with Artillery and Armored, in agreeing on that there was great closeness, too. Soon he was dozing, and I rested my head against the top of his, which was fine with him as well, the two of us secured by our mighty shock absorbers for the longer haul.

And so the reasons, like this great closeness and all the

others, were many and under ongoing excavation, which is to say that I was all the time still unearthing them. Still, these reasons were not causes—and much as hindsight might permit us to conflate them, they are not the same. As compared to these reasons, the cause was clearer in its formation, and simpler in its name: Avi, whom I loved, may his memory be a blessing.

Avi and I were born a month apart, I in May 1988 and he in June with his identical twin, Yoav, raised in Santa Barbara, California, the same Jewish community glue. Though the twins were American-born, they held Israel close, going there often and bringing home stories to share, forming a point of proximity to Israel for me and other children who had not grown a proximity of our own. In 2006, the twins moved to Israel to enlist in the army at eighteen, and when the Second Lebanon War broke out the same summer, I felt a faint little tug from the newspaper headlines—but I was set to start at Brown in the fall, so I thought of the twins who were beginning in Israel, and I prepared for freshman year.

The next faint Israeli tug came spring of 2009, an unexpected call from an excited Avi. He was finishing his service and had been admitted to Brown, and would start in the fall as I began my senior year. In August, we moved him into his freshman double and draped a great Israeli flag on his side of the room, before anything had announced itself on the other. He smoothed its corners with a reverence that made me sheepish, and then we sat with the Hebrew music on and the coffee brewing, for the stories he had brought home like the times before.

Once his dorm had filled, we would escape instead to the campus bar, where his eighteen-year-old cohorts could not follow, and it was there we were like rediscovered children learning wide-eyed from one another of the past three years. Avi was unsure if he could have a normal college experience.

He was older than most freshmen, and he had been a special forces trainer in counterterrorism tactics. Moreover, his heart was still in Israel. He showed me photos of himself grinning in fatigues, heading a squad of masked men in black body armor, and added that as some consolation he was reprising his role with the Providence city SWAT team, where he had agreed to lead training for hostage situations. He was an uncommon commodity, it seemed to me over the bar table, which was perhaps the same reason he insisted he had everything to learn from me, placed great value on my campus expertise, which was a common commodity of just the kind he needed.

And so we kept up our close and uneven exchanges, and Avi soon became a companion I had not known I needed, a friendship different from my others at school, without the rules of engagement that had been written into them. And I adored not only his new stories but his new form, because I was awed by what he had become since leaving home at eighteen. He returned with presence that made women fling themselves at him, authority that made peers listen when he spoke, clarity that made them stay. He made waves on campus as an ambassador for Israel, working for the inclusive dialogues he saw as foundational to peace. It was at another Shabbat dinner at Hillel, where we ate together each week, that he shared he had been tapped to help design a Brown course on the Israeli-Palestinian conflict including narratives from both sides. He peppered me for ideas for the course and I said I would reflect, though I left dinner reflecting mainly on looking forward to his company again, knowing it would replenish me, and make me feel safe. Avi was in vivid motion, and to be at close proximity to this motion set me alight. I treasured what I learned from him, and knew there was so much I would learn from him still.

And so I cried out on Friday, February 12, 2010, when I woke up late in the morning, sat at my computer, and found his name in small letters across my screen. I looked away and back at the screen to find still displayed our college president's email announcement that early this morning, Avi had been struck and killed by a drunk driver while walking home to his dorm.

I reread the sentence, continued to the next, where the president wrote that Avi had been a young man of inordinate strength and integrity, raced through the text for the words that would change the story, give evidence of a different ending. The concluding words, instead, advised of the availability of grief counselors, and that those wishing to gather in Avi's memory were encouraged to join at Hillel.

The letter had ended at Hillel and so that was where I would find the answer, where the story would resolve. I took a coat and stepped into the premature winter, and as I began, my hope failed, feet slipped, and I stumbled over the hard ice on the sidewalk, hood flipped over my face to hide the world from my eyes. From underneath I saw only the sidewalk and the boots and legs passing me, and grew enraged at the faceless legs for how they chattered and laughed. But though I was confused, and enraged, my tears had not yet overtaken me on my path. Not until I came to the Hillel doors, where Avi had greeted me only last Friday, and where on this Friday I found all the others who, like me, had gathered to mourn him.

Monday, we gathered in Los Angeles for Avi's funeral. We formed a circle around his grave, where Yoav stood alone, gazing down over it, toes curled over its edge. Beside the grave a great mound of unearthed soil, and planted within it a wooden shovel, so that each mourner in turn could take hold of the shovel, and turn with it to the grave.

Once our circle was whole, there was a long moment it remained unbroken. Then the shovel's path began, each mourner finding its shaft in his hands and stepping to the mound of earth, then letting his soil fall into the grave below. My attention fixed first on the shovel—hard backbone, metal head, the earth it gathered and spilled. There was comfort in finding that the shovel was master of ceremony: the rest of our circle was lifeless, was gray and still, except where it came. And I watched it grip each new mourner who found it on him, his palms opening as it neared.

But my attention soon turned to the casket below, clumps of soil falling from the sky above, fresh and airy soil unlike the dense earth that bordered the grave on all four sides. From my place several paces back from the grave, I could not see the whole casket but only the farthest quarter, where I understood Avi's feet to be. I longed to stand closer, to see the whole before it was gone beneath the falling earth. Then I raised my eyes back to the shovel winding through the circle, bringing life to each it touched, and found relief it would soon bring me forward.

My eyes returned to Avi's feet below, to the wood that protected them. I saw now how meager were our spurts of soil; despite our exertion, how many more of our heaves it would take to fill the grave. And there was no impatience now to step into full view of the casket, to the whole of its length. Gone now my longing to see it, gone my relief that the shovel would pull me to where it waited. Now, tearing myself from our gray circle, I ran alone, ripping the gray fabric of my mourner's suit from my skin as I fled, running to a place where all around was loud and not quiet, far from vision of the quarter casket.

But then my eyes rose again from where they had come to rest, and the shovel was nearly upon me. My legs rooted where they stood, palms opened and swelled.

And then it was Avi's wedding day. And his bride so beautiful in her white, and they gleamed in their chairs and

I ran in with the others and we seized the wooden legs of his chair and then heaved him up high and blood raced through my limbs and I laughed as he bounced at the top of our heave and the soil flew from my chair leg and I gripped the wood harder and heaved again and more earth flew and the others were gone and I alone with the hard wooden shaft of my shovel and with every heave fell the soil onto my tears to seal them there, in the earth, with him.

5.

On my wrist a bright ribbon, reading "Seek Peace and Pursue It," the words of a psalm Avi had held dear. In the main hall of Hillel with others who wore the same ribbon, reading stories from the library upstairs, snowing outside and the furnace on. The place that in the days after his death we could go at any hour and be found by others who had come for the same reason. Our second place was the off-campus house of Megan, one of us, a bright and spacious place she offered for gathering, which became another place not like the others, one shielded from the chattering boots and legs outside.

A spell I could not have preserved on my own but one we held for one another, one that made the time flow milky sweet, kept Avi less far, and made me feel safe. It was in this protected space, with the ribbons in the room, that it occurred to me I would join the army, like Avi had done. On the walk home from Hillel, it changed things, because it straightened the edges that were blurred, and it was the middle of the week because I remembered now the classes I had missed today and the ones I had been going to miss tomorrow. It was a strange way of being snapped from a dream, but I found my feet moving home faster on the compacted earth, and when I woke the next day, I jumped from bed as I had not done in a while.

I called my parents in the afternoon to talk them through, after I had first gone back to Hillel, where the furnace was on. I bounded upstairs to the cold second floor, and from an empty room found my mother's number, and began to march down the floor as it rang. She answered at the start of my second stride and I asked if she could get Dad on the line, too. His voice came before the end of the room, and I told them.

It's your grief speaking, said Mom, and of course it is, I replied. I turned to pace back the length of the room, and you should cool off before a decision like this, she said, and that was the thing I knew I should not do, I said, marching faster, because what a waste to make a choice you only think is right, when you had once, with all of yourself, known it was. Dad said he supported the decision, though he would have to think about whether he agreed with that reasoning, and I said I would think about that part, too, but not the decision, and I thanked him. And I wanted the decision done, set in stone while I still knew it was right and before I came to only think it was. So as soon as we hung up, I descended to the warm room where my friends were gathered, and began telling them, too.

In the days after, my sleep returned, routine restored itself, and I set about preparing. As a child I had learned to read the letters in my prayer books, but I spoke hardly a word of Hebrew so I took a stack of books from the library and started over with the alphabet. I resolved to reach the best shape of my life, and now spent afternoons running sprints in the field, faster than I had been before Avi's death, because I knew why I was there. But then, why I was there was not for him. It felt good to think and say so, decisive, as though I had found a way to answer a thing I could not. But there was more honesty in seeing this was no answer, and that what it meant was I was not doing it for him. That that was only a neighbor to the truth.

"What do I do with his number on my phone?"

Through a benefactor's generosity, Hillel had arranged the round-trip flights of all students who wished to attend the funeral, free of charge. A second email had come while we were in California, encouraging us to use the professional grief counselors Brown had made available. I made a note, deleted the email, and once back from the funeral, I wrote to my most trusted professor, David Josephson, who taught music. I asked if he could see me on an urgent basis and he welcomed me the same afternoon.

"If you are asking," he replied, "then you're not prepared to do anything but keep the number. Not today, but some other day you'll find his name there again and know to let it fall away like a leaf from a tree."

That day seemed far, I said. Sometimes I would rest my phone in both palms like a book, and reread our messages, from the first one recorded up through the last. Consider sending a message back, or even calling. Return to early Friday morning, wonder if I called, he would stop to answer, or pause, arrive five seconds later to the street. The professor listened, and at the end of our session asked if I wished to meet again soon. After my decision, I returned again, and told him, and said I was doing it for Avi, like I had been saying to others even though it was only a neighbor to the truth.

"You are not doing it for Avi. You are doing it because of Avi."

I stayed silent, ready to assent to what he would explain next, but he had a request instead.

"I won't try to change your mind, but I want you to remember the nonlinear and weaving ways of grief."

6.

If there was a time to try ecstasy, it was now, so I accepted a baggie from my friends, two capsules within, and tucked it in my shoe as we headed to the college's Main Green for the Friday show. It was Spring Weekend, Brown's annual spring saturnalia, and today we had Major Lazer and MGMT playing on the Green. It had always been the best weekend of the year, even in the three years before without amphetamines in my shoes. I felt a tickle of relief when the guard at the gate waved me down with his wand and let me through, gait just a bit suspect, foot still curled in protection of the capsules beneath.

We threw down our picnic blankets on the lawn, then together pulled our treats from their hiding places, swallowed, and continued as we were. I took one to start and put the second back in my shoe, and the lawn was filling all the way up with bright faces and before long the grass had grown extravagantly lush beneath me, and then my shoes and socks were tossed to the blankets for my feet to envelop themselves in the earth that held them. The others had lost their shoes, too, and we roved between the stage and our blanket outpost, seething with the need to hold on to one another and drink in every magic raindrop falling onto us. In some discovered oasis there we lay on our blankets, bellies and limbs in a heap on the soft earth, and a photographer for the college yearbook happened by. I looked up at him from where my head rested on another's hot thigh, his face framed in white light against the sky, mouthing in tune with the music that he would love to take a picture. I nodded, so eager to remember this moment, so glad it would be recorded, and smiled up at the sky above, my open shoe lying next to my face on the grass, the second capsule still sitting within beaming for the yearbook, too.

After the show ended, we caught word that Major Lazer was setting up at Megan's house off campus, for a late-night encore. We picked up our things and made it minutes or hours later to Megan's, where Major Lazer's bass still pulsed down the city block. I walked into the house, its hardwood floor lush and pillowy beneath my feet, bass thudding up through it and into the core of me. I had not been back inside this house since my last time sitting in it as a grief refuge, a place we held one another in raw mourning and in quiet, streaming tears. The rooms now throbbed with electric pulses and sweaty young bodies and I, one more among them, veins bursting with life, continued then to dance, heartbeat linking back up to the rhythm in the floorboards and the air.

7.

It was like a drug to see the Green this way, colors warmer than in any of our four years. Tonight was Campus Dance, the ball of commencement weekend, on the same Green we knew—but now colored gold underneath the lanterns running in the sky across its length, painting the grass beneath our feet. It was our farewell party, but also a reunion for graduates of years past, and a time for all of us to sing the alma mater song.

We arrived with a couple glasses already in us, and there were full bars at the corners of the Green to pour us more. I got a glass of wine to hold and walked onto the lawn, because my family had come to meet me and I was sure to find them here. My friend Ken joined and we went together under the lanterns, and paused in the middle to breathe it in, our glasses coming to rest on the tall white table beside us. Across the table was another wineglass and behind it a new face, and I gave myself a bubbly introduction to Tarek, whose name tag said he was an alumnus of 2003. He was a lawyer now at a big firm called Covington and Burling and was thrilled to be back on campus, and was witty and collected despite the flushes in his cheeks, too. I told him I was thinking about law school, and I listened with interest as he told me about Covington and provided his card.

Then he asked what I planned after graduation, and I said I had decided to join the Israeli army. He did not ask why, but if I was ready, and it was the first time anyone had asked. A question I was not prepared for, and "No, he is not" came Ken's laughing answer from beside me, almost done with his glass of dark red. And an answer had been voiced now and not one I could contest with a straight face, so instead of speaking to cover for myself, I raised my glass again to my lips, to cover them that way instead.

"*L'chaim* to our brave volunteer!"

I emptied my glass and set it down, cheeks already flushed in the sparkle of the Shabbat table my hosts had set. Eli and Chaya were two of the first people I met in Israel, and they insisted on being the only ones I would need. In the weeks before my September flight to Tel Aviv, I had combed my family's network for Israeli contacts, sending signals through the airwaves for anyone who might catch me as I landed and prepared to enlist. The search was a short one: once my call had reached Eli in Jerusalem, he answered with a note that he would refuse to let me look any further. And so Eli—a family friend twice removed who had not ever known my name—took me in and gave me warmth, light, and shelter befitting a native son.

Eli's son Shachar had served in an elite reconnaissance unit, and Eli spoke of Shachar's service with quiet and immense pride. Shachar was now a grown man, living nearby in Jerusalem with his wife and his own infant son—but still framed in gold on the house's walls were images of him from that earlier time, a handsome teenager with a dark red beret tilted across his brow. Eli paused with me in front of each one, hands resting behind his back, inviting me to go for a swim in what I saw. There in the hall, I began to make sense of why he had so generously taken me as his own. He had heard in my call some echo, foreign to me until its first whisper came as we stood together, Shachar's young eyes looking back at us from behind the golden frame.

These first weeks in a strange land, I was every way an infant and Eli my proud father. He spent unhurried evenings with me at the fireplace, eager to suffuse me with Israeli color in the short time he knew was left before my induction. He shared Israeli art and stories, and read me poetry, in the original Hebrew and his own translation.

So one night he read to me a favorite, Yehuda Amichai's "A Man in His Life." Two times over: verse by verse, first the Hebrew, followed by his English.

A man doesn't have time in his life to have time for everything.
He doesn't have seasons enough to have a season for every purpose.
Ecclesiastes was wrong about that.

His translated verse was slow, and easy, though he paused to ask how to say *Kohelet* ("Ecclesiastes"). Eli's English was the ideal level: good, not fluent. Any more mastery on his part and there might have risen anxiety in our silences, a compulsion to speech, a need to probe and to question and discuss, the way adults do. Instead I had the luxury to sit, and enjoy the beautiful things he gave me, to learn through senses and not words, the way an infant would.

A man needs to love and to hate at the same moment, to laugh and cry with the same eyes, with the same hands to throw stones and to gather them, to make love in war and war in love.

And to hate and forgive and remember and forget, to arrange and confuse, to eat and to digest, what history takes years and years to do.

I was stunned: Eli's English could be flawless, when he needed.

A man doesn't have time. When he loses he seeks, when he finds he forgets, when he forgets he loves, when he loves he begins to forget.

As Eli knew, I understood almost nothing of the Hebrew,

like any infant not yet answering his father's words and nonetheless absorbing every one of them.

And his soul is seasoned, his soul is very professional. Only his body remains forever an amateur. It tries and it misses, gets muddled, doesn't learn a thing, drunk and blind in its pleasures and in its pains.

He will die as figs die in autumn, shriveled and full of himself and sweet, the leaves growing dry on the ground, the bare branches already pointing to the place where there's time for everything.

Afternoons, Eli would walk me through Jerusalem's colorful Machane Yehuda outdoor market, each of my senses alight, and buy me fresh fruit to eat as we walked, and bread to take home for the evening. He would bring me to his favorite merchants, and each of them would beam at the sight of him and welcome him in. He would introduce me to them as his brave new soldier, and I would blush and shake their eager hands, find growing assurance in telling them in Hebrew how wonderful it was to meet them. In turn, they would thank me for the service they knew I had yet to begin, throw me extra apples or refuse Eli's money for my food altogether, because it was the least they could do.

Most insistent of all was Eli's friend and favored falafel master Itai. On the warm Friday I met him, all the market pulsed in the last hours before closing for Shabbat, and I was carrying the great braided challah Eli had bought for home. Eli told me I was about to taste Jerusalem's best falafel, and he led me through the calm center of the plaza as bright vegetables and pastries and echoes flew all along its length behind. There, in the last stall on our left was Itai, packing and slinging spirited falafels to a crowd of customers from behind the counter.

Like the others, Itai opened warmly at the sight of Eli, and lit up behind the counter as Eli told him my name. Itai sliced open a warm brown pita and started filling it to brimming, and I knew as he began that he would not consider payment for it. He stuffed the pita with love and began to stretch out his arm to hand it to me. Then he paused, pulled it back to cram a couple last golden falafel balls into its seams, and offered it again with a prayer: "For strength on the road ahead."

Itai, of course, did not ask me for one shekel. Nor ever did Eli for any part of his kindness. But in accepting it, and in enjoying the gifts and praise of his friends and the others I met, and remembering the way their smiles lingered on me as I turned to walk on, I was beginning to undertake a debt of a new kind.

8.

"Do you ever have homicidal thoughts, fantasies?"
"No."

His question and my answer came in English, even though he was the army doctor performing my medical fitness exam, and even though the charts on his clipboard indicated my body parts were Hebraic without exception. Because I knew how to say a Hebrew "no," but only a polite prepubescent one, and would have had no vocabulary for such a bold-faced denial.

Despite my hours memorizing verb charts through summer, the discovery I was not fluent had taken no longer than to board the El Al plane at LAX, the seating instructions barking unintelligibly from the speakers, leaving me gripping my case in the aisle, hoping for a kind English voice to follow. And so I understood that I was master of verb tables and moron in speech, and that there was no substitute for long months of words pouring into my ears and out, building tightly funded neuron routes like a westward railroad.

"Have you ever done hard drugs?"

"No," I lied, and I began to wonder if they might make polygraphs more unbeatable by forcing you to deny your accusations in a foreign language. Because I had produced this word, too, with an ease that seemed to satisfy him at least of my answer, if not its truth.

Next I arched my feet slightly, like I might if I had drugs stashed underneath. I had heard a flat-foot diagnosis was a killer on the medical exam, so I posed with my best arch in show. He slid an orthotic under each foot and seemed satisfied, humming along to the next item on the test. And I squinted during the vision test to help my nearsighted right eye comprehend the writing on the wall, but he was forgiving there, too.

"*M'tzuyan* (Excellent)," he remarked at the end of his list. He would not have switched back to Hebrew to give bad news. "*Tishim v'sheva!*"

An army doctor was rarely in the business of giving better news than this, because this meant 97, the highest possible fitness rating. When I had asked Eli earlier why the scale peaked at 97, he replied that a 97 is a 100 who has had his *brit milah* (circumcision) and is on his way to manhood, and now I could not wait to tell him how I had grown. He would remind me that a 97 qualified me physically for any unit, including special forces like Shachar's, even though Eli knew my wish was to serve in the infantry's ranks and files. For that, an 82 would have sufficed—but no less I held these 15 bonus points like a prize, to know I had been stamped as a model of imperfection.

But there were other hurdles still to clear today at my *Tzav Rishon* ("First Order"), my day of being poked and rated at the recruitment bureau, and the last hoop to jump through toward my first day in uniform. I had made it without incident through the others, starting at the address listed on the Ministry of Defense website, where I arrived at the second floor of a beige office building to a locked metal door. I knocked, rehearsed once more my announcement that I was here to join the army, and delivered it to the tired kid who answered. He slumped onto the door and watched, waited for me to go away instead of volunteer for what he was condemned to, three years playing gargoyle at the first metal door. But I stood and said no more because I hoped not to reveal I had rehearsed just this one line, and after a silence eyeing me like a fly he could not be bothered to swat, he let me in and provided English versions of the forms. Next the Ministry of the Interior for my visa, and the Jewish Agency for a stamp on my rabbi's letter authenticating my Judaism, and with these I reported back to the Ministry of Defense, at last rewarded with a date for this *Tzav Rishon*, this point of no return.

I had enlisted through *Machal*, which was an acronym for *Mitnadvim Chutz La'aretz* ("Volunteers from Outside the Land"), a pathway to army service for noncitizens. A Machal enlistee served just eighteen months, starting with a three-month *ulpan*, a language immersion boot camp to prepare him for both the language and the uniform of service. But some had it even better, because those able to ace the Hebrew exam skip the *ulpan*, and serve just fourteen months instead.

I had no delusions of passing this exam, so I walked into the room at ease and sat down with the tester, a soldier with silver pins that gleamed on her shirt from beneath her long brown hair, which fell on both sides of her buttons. She handed me the sheet and she had liquid brown eyes and told me to take my time. I scanned the page and lit up, because this was that pasteurized textbook Hebrew I had already acquired, and she smiled when I looked up and she had smooth olive skin and I knew all of these words. And their past and present and future selves, and though she had not rushed me, I began filling the sheet on a mission, and returned it to her, because I was excited to get to the oral portion.

She began with a blur, and I had watched her lips but not heard what came from them, so I asked her to come again and now I heard: "How many brothers and sisters do you have?"

"Two brothers one sister," I reported without garnish, because I was thrilled to be on the scoreboard, and her mouth curled up and she made a little note with her pen, and I blushed to imagine what it might have said. Then she spoke but again a blur, in and out without landing.

"*Slichah* (Excuse me)?"

And she made a second note and it felt as though she was

testing me, so I tuned in close, and when she spoke again, it was, of course, to ask how long I had lived here.

"Three weeks," I stated, because that was how long it had been since the plane landed. She seemed to like this because she asked what I liked most about life here after three weeks, and this got me going because there was so much, and now she had put down her pen to listen, and she had put her hand in her hair instead. By now I had forgotten the exam, which I had no delusions of passing anyway, so I told her about Machane Yehuda and the warm people and the yellow sunsets over Jerusalem from Eli's house in the hills. And where I had no words, she spoke them for me, and I nodded because her words were the same ones in my heart, and she nodded back.

And when I stood up to go, I wished I could have stayed, and I waved to her on the way out, and her smile stayed on me as I walked out the door. Outside it was warm and there were soft and pretty clouds in the sky, and I started my way home to Eli's. When he opened the door to welcome me, I began to tell him about her, before it came to me that I had never gotten her name.

It was the next week, Thursday, October 28, I was at home reading through one of Eli's Hebrew picture books when my black Nokia's screen lit up, and Eli was in the other room, and no one had the number of my black Nokia except Eli and them. It could still have been a wrong number, but now on the line came a hard voice who seemed sure it was not.

"*Slichah?*" I said, because I had not been spoken to this way before, but instead of an easier Hebrew came equally abrupt English.

"Mazel tov on passing your Hebrew test."

"What?"

"Your place to report is *Givat HaTachmoshet* on Monday, November first, by eight o'clock."

"Thank you."

"*B'hatzlacha* (Good luck)," and she was gone, and I had not meant to thank her or let her go because I did not know a *Givat HaTachmoshet*, the part of her command she had not stopped to anglicize.

"Ammunition Hill!" Eli beamed after I had passed light-headed to the next room. "A famous memorial site from the Six-Day War. That's just four days away, let me take you to see it first before you have to go."

She had passed me. My olive-skinned tester had filled in my words for me and on top of it passed me, and even though I did not know her name, I told Eli this, too.

"It must make you want to kiss her." He smiled, and in the moment I agreed. But then we went to Ammunition Hill in the afternoon, and walked through the trenches and Eli regaled me with the lore of the men who had died here for the land, and that evening I sat with him wondering if the test results could be appealed. We talked awhile, in English, about how exciting it was that I would start basic training in November, not March, and how fast I would learn. Then he flipped on the TV, and laughed along with the disembodied faces on the screen, their words hurtling past me, impervious to any "*Slichah?*" I might have mouthed their way.

9.

The next afternoon I was reading in the yard where it overlooked Jerusalem, and when the light started going yellow, I put down my book to see the city turn to gold. Once I heard music from inside the house, I knew Eli and Chaya were home to decorate the table in Sabbath gold, too. After we sat to eat, he brought out a special bottle and raised a *l'chaim* to what was ahead. The wine was warm on my lips and the table glowed, and after dinner I went to bed the happiest I had been since the plane landed just a month before. And in the morning when I came downstairs, they were there waiting, and had set out fresh figs for us from the neighbor's tree.

But that night I dreamed of getting on the bus all alone, and when I awoke Sunday, they had gone to work and I was on my own. I began preparing for the bus tomorrow, and it was not until evening that Eli came home, then said he had almost forgotten it was time to cut my hair. He was right, I would need a tight buzz tomorrow and my hair had not been touched since I arrived, so he led me to the bathroom and sat me in front of the mirror.

Among Orthodox Jews, an infant boy's hair is permitted to grow until he is three years old. Then it is time for his *upsherin*, his first haircut, the ritual signaling his transition from infancy to the start of his education. I was not Orthodox and neither was Eli, but now he began to sing softly, for the two of us together in the closed room, as he turned on the buzzer and leaned my head over the sink. He had seen I was afraid of tomorrow, but I was calm now as he stood over and sang to me, holding the buzzer in one hand and my shoulder in the other, and his song continued as I watched the sink begin to fill with thick blond clumps of hair. Above was the mirror, but I did not want to see myself or him before I was ready, so I kept my eyes in the sink until the buzzing ended, then his song, and it was time for me to stand and for my hair to begin to regrow.

In the morning Eli drove me to Ammunition Hill and snapped a photo of me leaving home, wide smile, baby-white scalp, bag slung low on my back before turning to go. On Thursday he had brought me down to the old battle site and told of the men he knew who had fought there, but today I went alone into the new museum above. Inside there were exhibits for tourists, and miniature clay models of the trenches we had walked through below. I was early for the bus so I began reading the exhibit signs printed side by side in Hebrew and English, blocking out the English side and forcing myself to try the other, and I had made it through a couple when I saw the bus was outside and other boys were starting to board.

I was unsure whether the others boarding were Israeli or foreign like me, but as the bus pulled onto the street half-full, we were quiet and did not sound like boys close to home. It felt the way I had dreamed it a couple nights ago, and we had filled the window seats and left all the neighboring aisle seats empty, and since there was no one beside me to talk to, I looked out the window, like the boy on the far side of the aisle was doing, too.

It did not seem long before the bus rolled into Bakum, the base Eli had told me about. The army's recruit processing base near Tel Aviv, not the base that made soldiers but the one that gave them things to carry. Bakum could not have done both of these, could not have been the one to throw the things upon you and then grind them into you. It was enough for it to do the first half of this work, which was the more invasive and the harder to forgive, so that we could begin the second half somewhere clean.

Bakum pushed itself through your skin and into your bloodstream, with the compulsory inoculations that waited in the clean white nursing room. Bakum gave you a new seven-digit name, a *mispar ishi*, which meant "personal number" and made no apologies for that contradiction. Bakum engraved this name onto your two new dog tags, one to string around your neck and the other to break in half, one half in each boot for alternate identification if anything should disfigure the one above. Bakum stripped away your other jewelry from before, so that you would not have to hold this violence against your commanders, who would be spared this first half of the work, so that they could begin the second.

And when we filed out of the bus, there was no drill sergeant waiting for us, so we milled around for thirty minutes in front of the building, kicking rocks in the yard. It was where we had been let off and no one seemed ready to try going elsewhere, so we stayed, silence broken now and then by our little rocks hitting big ones or the building's walls, before a green uniform opened the door to wave us in. This came as a relief in a way it would not have if they had let us in right away, so we huddled together, grateful from our first step into the building. I hoped not to have to speak so I wadded myself into the middle of our procession, away from its exposed front or back, as we entered and waited to be received.

Inside there were still no drill sergeants but men in clean uniforms, who signaled us forward to line up for the first room, which was the portrait room for your new ID. I smiled for the camera and accepted the card they gave me, and the dog tags they gave me in the room after. And in another room was the nurse with the injections, to ensure we would all have these in common, too, and we progressed through the rooms in our same neat line, which was still spaced apart a bit as we had done on the bus, and we still did not say much, even as we were coming to resemble one another more and more along the way. Until the last room, where we were ready now to step into the same clean uniform the others wore while they had led our way.

An empty locker room, where there were no more green uniforms but the factory-sealed ones they had piled in our arms. It was quiet and the line had stopped moving, and because they had not said what else to do, we began to look at the things we carried. Some of us began to open them, then the rest of us, and then our neat line split apart and we were tearing at the plastic wrap and shedding it on the floor, and the boy ahead of me had ripped out his new pants and was rushing to get into them so I hurried with my own. As my buttons flew, I avoided looking up at the mirrors on the walls, as I had done while Eli cut my hair, and now there were men who were fully dressed and running out the door, and it was the next door so I laced my boots and ran to follow.

Outside was a man who stood waiting for us, and we formed a row to face him, and I made it into the middle as the last men found their way out to the light. I was glad not to be one of them, and we stiffened as he began to walk in front of our row, because now anyone could see there were three stripes on his sleeves and none on ours. They had not told us where to put our hands, and to my left were butler hands behind the back and to my right fig leaves in front, and I had settled on leaves when the man stopped in front of me, looked at them. I switched to butler hands but his eyes stayed, and he was not looking at my hands but next to them, at the edge of my shirt, spilling out loose over my pants where I had rushed to fasten them. It was the way I learned that, on *aleph*, one tucks in his pants.

Me, frozen, first defect off the assembly line. I raised my eyes and braced but was relieved to find him still calm, holding out a black garbage bag. He pointed me back to the locker room and I understood without further explanation, to gather the strewn plastic, forgotten T-shirts, debris of our panicked metamorphosis. And so I returned to the room bag in hand, my campaign of Israeli garbage cleanup to begin in earnest.

"Welcome to bitch duty." This caught me off guard, because I had begun filling my bag and thought myself alone in the room, before the voice came in unaccented English.

"How did you know I was American?" I looked up and responded to the other one there, who wore the same new green and held another black bag.

"You made it obvious, dude."

Adam was a volunteer like me, and a college graduate (Babson, where he studied business). Unlike me, a good command of Hebrew and a surer sense of how he came to be a trash collector in a foreign locker room. I assumed he had been ordered here because he was defective, too, and I was glad for that, and we took a while in the dim room together, speaking English and gathering Hebrew garbage before exiting with our full bags into the hard daylight.

We rejoined the others and were ready to ship to the remote northern base of Michve Alon, the other base Eli had described in the car this morning. Bakum was for everyone, but Michve just for us foreigners. Michve, he had told me with a twinkle in his rearview as I dozed in the backseat, was to catch us up on what we had missed in the past eighteen years. Michve was a kindness, because it would be cruel to drop us in basic training alongside natives without a small head start. And so we were given three weeks at Michve to dress up as soldiers, for the only reason anyone plays dress-up, to help imagine the real thing. Like a three-week Purim holiday, he explained, which was a sweet vision and the one he ended with as we had nearly made it to Ammunition Hill.

I began telling Adam what I knew of Michve, but he knew about it, too—he had heard from a friend of his who made it through before. Michve was a brutal three-week boot camp, he explained, which we had to survive to earn the right to be called soldiers and begin basic; in the meantime dressing for the jobs we wanted, in uniforms not yet earned, affronts to the eyesight of officers who could not believe our chutzpah to wear them. Michve's discipline was ruthless and its exit door wide open, so that by the time we made it through to basic, there would be no accidental arrivals; we had had three weeks beforehand to discover we had gotten on the wrong bus. This seemed different from how Eli had narrated it through the rearview, so I finished recounting that version to Adam, too, but since neither of us knew for sure, we left it there and sat waiting a few hot hours for the bus. When it came, the same commander ordered us to run to it before it left us behind, so I ran fast to keep up with the others, and as far as I could tell, we all made it aboard.

It was past nightfall when we landed at Michve Alon, a hundred and some kilometers into Israel's green north. This bus, too, had been quiet, even though no one had ordered us to be, and I had thought of little but to find these new sleeves stiff as cardboard on my arms, and to wonder what the rifle would feel like in them, too.

The bus stopped moving then, and it was dark. No one came aboard to tell us what to do, but once it was clear the engine was not starting again, a few of us stood up, then a few more, then we were moving quickly. We grabbed our things and hurried off the bus onto the coarse gravel, scuffing our new boots in the dark, then forward to the great concrete yard which awaited under the flood of white stadium lights from above.

There on the concrete was our first authority. He stood erect as we scrambled to collect ourselves, gathering to face him before he had said his first word, and I did not know his name, rank, or role, but the lights shone on him from all sides and cast him in shadowless white. His name was Shimon, and he would be the drill sergeant to our infant platoon—and so at last had come the drill sergeant, but still not the one I had imagined. The one in my dream had disparaged, scorned, screamed at me two inches from my face in words I could not answer. But Shimon, it came clear, would not rely on volume to convey his authority now or ever. Instead, he stood silent a long time, introducing himself with his image under the lights, stock-still but for the white tzitzit that hung at his four corners, swaying in the wind. These were the ritual fringes worn by observant men beneath their shirts, and I had seen them before but not like this, searing white, like pillars, framing his figure in the light.

Shimon was religious, then, which I understood was uncommon in the army. He had been born and bred in Kiryat Arba, a West Bank settlement on a hill above the city of Hebron. He was different from the other commanders I came under: secular men with not quite the same constellation of motives. In mornings I watched Shimon seclude himself, bind tefillin upon his arm, face due south to Jerusalem, and pray alone. He walked alone, too, and his tzitzit tailed in the air accentuating his gait, upright and with a crusading purpose.

It occurred to me he had been named for the Shimon of Genesis, wrathful second son of Jacob, who with his brother Levi, in retaliation for an affront to the family, laid waste to the Canaanite city of Shechem. This biblical Shimon would no longer be faceless to me. Now he would be the Shimon I knew: he of six-foot-two and boyish features, of short blond hair and freckles and stout shoulders, his rifle a native edge to his silhouette; who stood as we scrambled, who spoke with the spaces between his words.

He was not our ranking officer, but there was another reason my high authority was Shimon and no swaggering captain with more rage in his throat or stripes on his sleeve: his Hebrew was calm and lucid, did not ever crowd the air. He spoke in an elevated register that more closely resembled the textbook Hebrew I had learned in the summer, and had a way of adorning his speech with scripture, words resonant to me from longer ago than that. These reminded me of where I was, and were of comfort. There was one among them he favored, which never once fell redundant from his lips: "*lo l'fached klal.*" He spoke in reference to a rabbinic proverb, one I had sung and cherished as a child: "All the world is a very narrow bridge, and the most important thing is to have no fear at all."

10.

Of comfort, too, was the realization I was not the only one to fall through the cracks, the only illiterate infiltrator to the base. Every one of us had been stamped proficient in the language, but it became clear that more than one of us were deaf, dumb, and mute in this new discourse. These others, I identified by the way the same faces sought shelter in the middle of our formations, the way the men in front of us heard orders and moved, then us bounding after them as monkey-see, monkey-do baboons.

I took thrills in slamming into these wide-eyed illiterates in the center of our rows, together speechless in spirit and letter. Colliding our elbows and worlds, unable to form words to one another even if we'd been allowed, because his tongue was Russian and his Amharic, and because he the third was no better able than I to force coarse Hebrew from his flustered French lips. Idiots together, our Hebrew was a primitive code, a syntactically bankrupt set of short words and short phrases, a small and adaptable—but always small—conduit between far worlds. Apart from our uniforms, all else we had in common was that in this land we were others, and that this was our trial before being deemed fit to serve alongside the natives groomed in youth to wear these colors still stiff on our backs.

Yet it was not long before the first time I felt something like a soldier. It was the day we had our rifles thrust upon us, lined up on the steaming asphalt outside the armory, one by one forward to the window to have them slid across the counter into our bracing hands, by an armory tech too tired to laugh at us. Because we had not even yet earned the grace to be called soldiers and because each rule of the game had been calculated to remind us of this, we were given obsoleted rifles, Vietnam-era M16s, old US Army relics in the wrong museum. It was no secret to anyone these were the standard-issue arm of the hapless Vietnam draftee, that these smooth black rifles had seen some shit, still held a starring place in the heart of many a former owner, carried grains of Vietnamese sand deep in the cracks between polished grip and trigger. It seemed a perverse fate that these artifacts of trauma should end their own long lives in such a role; that these bloodied instruments would be our empty toy rifles as we dashed up and down the yard in unpracticed formation, playing soldier.

We took no vow over our rifles, no ceremony—because we were not yet soldiers and these weapons were not ours. That afternoon, though, some uncounted stretch of time after my palms felt the first sparks of hard static from the rifle landing in them, I found them sealing their grip upon it as I sprinted across the yard, one task I could perform nearly as well as a soldier of any other shade of fluency or skin. This was, I envisioned, something like the way a soldier would hold his weapon, the way this rifle remembered being held back in the red summer of its own life: soldier's first hand on the trigger and second on the notched handguard, sweat streaming from them down the length of its surface, fluid produced in equal parts by the searing daylight and his own halfway contained panic and disorientation; the rifle back and forth across his chest as he strode, clutching his rifle close because that's what he had, running because that's what one does. I did not know any of this, though. I was only a confused trainee, and so during a lull later the same afternoon, after the sun had crossed from its peak, I examined my rifle to see if it might fill in any of the blanks for me.

I found its words etched in English. That was a comfort.

The manufacturer, Colt Firearms. The serial number, a string of Anglo-Saxon digits. The safety switch and its settings of "SAFE," "SEMI," and "AUTO" engraved in bold at 9, 12, and 3 o'clock as times of day, a season for every purpose, save for the 6 o'clock that yawned, unmarked, underneath the others.

But then it had other markings, too, younger ones. Above the safety switch and innocuously to the left, out of reach of my thumb but before came the length of the barrel, five crude tally marks incised into the metal: four in parallel and a fifth slashed abruptly through the all of them. I sat with them, ran my finger over their edges. If only I were able to have carbon-dated these scars. I could conceive that the marks had been etched by some bored soldier or armory tech stranded on base, as a mockery, a cruel joke. I could conceive also that these marks on my rifle's surface originated in the same land as those grains of sand trapped for good down within it.

Long days, short weeks. This was how Chaim, one of few religious men among our number, had said it to God or to no one at all upon waking in the bunk above me on the cold Friday of our first week. Neither of us had yet had a week in these bunks, but I listened to him exhale after expelling the words and already they were true.

These first mornings awakening in the sagging womb of my bunk's metal webbing, there was a blurring of truth and dream, finding what my eyes awoke to just as surreal as what had fluttered past them while they slept before. It would be some time before this floundering part of my psyche, too, had been tamed, conquered, brought to heel; before I would begin days with calm acquaintance to the grainy world around me. But this first Friday, Chaim's words caught me in my metal womb, surfaced in my brain as though born within. It did not matter that he was their author, because they were mine, too;

they were correct as I reached to reclaim the rifle lying next to me, and I would subscribe to them. Cast into the dark, we clutch about, we seize upon our own dancing shadow and call it a pattern, we watch the world now bloom in harmony to that natural law. This was Chaim's, and I would decree it, too. I would not find him again after Michve Alon, but if I ever had, I'd have praised him for this code he prophesied from the heights of our bunk.

As my eyes opened all the way, I knew Chaim was up there on the far side of the thin brown cushion, because one of his four tzitzit hung down through the bunk's wretched metal weave, heavy with the week's filth, stained from its virginal white of Monday morning, four days ago, before the bus had taken him. The gray strings stirred and then rolled away out of sight above the cushion, and I knew it was time to move. Into dead center of the room had come Uri, platoon commander, already seething: "Two minutes," our allowance to be down in the yard dressed and in formation. I started the timer on my wristwatch, feet came to the floor, laces already flying. A minute fifty-four.

Even for this predawn hour it was frigid, a morning colder than the ones before, and I shivered in the yard, despite the blood hitting my feet and fingertips, the timer that had crept down to five before the last of us had stumbled out to the yard and into standing form. Uri took up his preferred speaking posture, which was to pace back and forth twelve inches from our front row, alternating quiet and thundering, mercy and ruthlessness, mixing their four permutations to avoid predictability, the most loathsome of weaknesses. This time, before reaching the end of the row, he pronounced—in a manner so barbaric, it rendered his meaning ambiguous—that we would see our families soon if all went well through morning.

He ceded the floor to Shimon, who stood at center without

a word while Uri threatened from behind, searching our rows for eyes to meet with. Though neither spoke, it was Shimon whose silence held the floor, waiting for our pulses to calm, his downward force on them firmer than Uri's pressing them back up. When we were ready, he led us toward the main concrete yard, alone out in front of our formation while Uri circled behind.

I marched toward Shimon's tall figure and away from Uri's, thankful to the dark for hiding my face from him, wincing at the blisters on my heels and the ache in the bones beneath. We made it up the hill to the main yard as the sun dawned, sending the center flagpole's shadow all the way across its length. And they spread us out in rows, because it was time for the Bar-Or, the physical fitness test: sit-ups, push-ups, and the two-kilometer run, each till exhaustion, to weigh and grade our vitality, to the full measure of what our bodies could generate.

The first two sets came easy, not yet awake enough for them to hurt. Instead dull background pain while the mind still slept, wringing out our reps by rote until each of us had collapsed in turn, and it was time for the run. Awake now in the full morning light, and they lined us up and let us go, staggering our start times in small groups, two kilometers around the base perimeter and back to where we began. I had not been on a real run since they brought us here, and now our shadows flew along the pavement in the cool morning air, gaining space from one another as we ran, and before long I was free even of the long shadow of the man behind me, farther alone now than I had been since we arrived. And along the way I came to realize I had forgotten my blisters and forgotten, for the first time, too, that I was running for them.

But we ran along the path they had marked for us, at the perimeter within the barbed wire, and even as I ran ahead, I was still behind the pack of men who were sent before. Michve

Alon was on a tall hill, so it was easy to see over the fence and onto the open green fields that stretched beyond, and glistened in the rain that had come last night, heavy on the roof over our bunks. And as we hugged the inside of the barbed wire, there came a point where I saw the fence dipped in height and drew in near the path where we ran, and I would not have had the thought but for how green the fields looked below but I was certain now, beyond doubt, that I could leap from the high point of the path and clear the fence, and keep running into the fields, to a place where I would no longer have to forget that I was running for them.

But another man's shadow had overtaken me now and my blisters stung again, now that I had remembered that I had forgotten them, and I received my numbers at the finish line after crossing in a clump of other men who were sent either after me or before. We joined the others exhausted on the concrete faceup under the sky, and I had forgotten my numbers already but there would be no cuts based on them anyway, not before basic training where they would make the cuts, not at Michve Alon where we would.

Last to cross was Saul, a round-faced Argentine who drew birds on his helmet, and Uri called formation before he could collapse with us on the concrete. Saul bent down heaving, and I stood in the row between him and Uri, who paced before us as Saul panted and sniffled from behind. Then his hard breath on my neck once he stood, and Uri paused in front of Saul, stared away from him at the others, the ones standing high and still, before inviting our return next week.

And we broke formation then, for a field lesson on rifle maintenance, on disassembling parts whose English names I would never learn, a forced march back to the armory to be relieved of our stained weapons, a salute, then a strange and tender walk out the gates back the way we had come. We emerged to a graphic blue sky, and to a shock and awe that these free skies had seen only four nights and days since we last left them in the bus's rearview fading to black.

There would be no army bus to take us back out, back home. Instead we gathered at the side of the highway to wait for the rural bus route that rumbled by every twenty minutes, our release staggered by the commanders in controlled waves, to do us one last violence for the week; to prove that our freedom, too, would be rationed to us; to deny us a real exodus; to subjugate even as they freed. Secondary to these, to ensure no passing bus would be overwhelmed, its windows clawed, that we would do no violence to one another in our haste to board. Because we were here to harness our violence, not expel it, and because they held monopoly over its exercise. Because there would be a bus only once in a while, and on each one only so many rides home.

I made it out with a couple dozen other numbered men, assured enough of making it on the next bus, and sat down on the rocks on the far side of the open road. There across the way from the bus stop, in the valley below Michve Alon in a place I could not have seen on our way in, was a lush and rolling military cemetery. I did not know how old the cemetery was, whether it had come to be there before or after the base, which Israeli poet had decided to make the younger of the two a neighbor to the first, of all the fertile ground to choose from in the land's beautiful north. But from where I sat, buckling under an undisguised culling of those not suited for combat, fatigued in my body and throat, looking from the far side of the civilian highway back at the green burial ground and the gray fortress on a hill above, I could find no insult in his design.

When the bus's green roof appeared on the horizon, I stood and fell in line behind the others, at last feeling safe at our formation's exposed tail, and stepped onto the bus for my first time flashing my army ID to ride free, and for my second time feeling something like a soldier. There was one more open window seat at the back, and I fell onto it, sprawling my legs over the aisle seat while I could. After the engine was up to speed, a softer sound came from the seat in front of mine: another trainee's headphones rested in his lap, a melody rising from them as his head lay inert against the window, unconscious somewhere between play and listen. Leona Lewis's "Bleeding Love." I leaned back, her sweet voice faint enough to feel like home, hopeful he had set the song on replay. I don't believe I found out, because I recall instead the way her serenade cradled me to oblivion, my head limp against the window and bobbing in rhythm as the glass shuddered on the highway.

11.

Saul and some others were missing from formation the next week. Uri appeared pleased with this. Shabbat had come and gone, a petrifyingly abundant supper on Eli's table in Jerusalem. I ate sweet challah, and joined his *l'chaim* to my first week, and went out of my way to name M16 firing pins and other fresh Hebrew words. And retreated then to my borrowed bedroom to seal the shades over the windows, for a blackness undamaged by the streetlights outside, and slept for what I remembered of the weekend.

The weekend, of course, ends Sunday. The cruelest day of the week, not the Lord's Day but *Yom Rishon* ("First Day"), a peasant of a day, to be named in simple succession with the five days after, until the asylum of the seventh, the only one fit to be named. *Shabbat*, derived from the Hebrew root "to sit." To rest.

But for each Shabbat comes an after-Shabbat. So foreboded the favored refrain of Uri: *"L'kol Shabbat yesh Motzei Shabbat."* To confront us with how fleeting is our refuge, how gross a foolishness we would commit in indulging in real rest on this day, in pretending evening's shadow did not hang on the far side of every breath. Words served cold with the sinking orange light of Saturday afternoon. Worse, *Motzei Shabbat* comes not Sunday morning but Saturday night, the last throes of the sun swallowed by the horizon, when three pale stars in the night sky signal dawn of *Yom Rishon*, a day of no immunity under God.

This was the theme of Uri's speech to us in the waning daylight of the next Saturday, after they had detained us on base. After our Friday sunup formation, in front of which Uri had paced the yard in a controlled rage, revealing in his quiet-ruthless permutation (his favorite of the four) that the cooks were preparing our Shabbat dinner. After a long Friday, our dinner cooking in the kitchen and we in the sun, deepening our farmer's tans as we ran through shooting drills, Uri naming our weaknesses, impotent as the empty rifles we carried. After they had treated us to Shabbat dinner, which, as some relief, would not pass for any man's final meal. After we had been left alone for Saturday, declared free, as though our worlds spilled forth with liberties other than to fall unconscious on our metal bunks or under the stark shade of the barracks in the yard. After all of these, it was in the final hour of daylight that Uri resurfaced to menace the yard. Unhinged by the sight of our sloth; not yet authorized to assemble us; able, nonetheless, to sing to us these barbed words, this inverse lullaby. *L'kol Shabbat, yesh Motzei Shabbat.*

And so the final third star in the sky above brought the final of our weeks at Michve Alon. Our first formation of Saturday night looking crisp and ready under the lights, in spite of us. My heavy boots working creases into their leather, the moleskin I had brought back from Eli's house comforting my healing blisters from the week before. Uri's tirades and Shimon's sermons coming, grain by grain, into higher fidelity, more words catching in my webbing, fewer soaring past and swallowed by the air behind. My Vietnam M16, still empty, but feeling like my hands had grown some sense for how to hold it, one they might remember when it was gone.

In this last week it came as a surprise that before leaving these relics we would be permitted to fire them. I had resigned myself to wondering whether these even worked, whether they had trusted us with more than props, what it would feel like to pull the trigger, how the rifle would quake, how it would feel in my hands then.

Before Michve Alon, I had not touched a gun, much less fired one, so I had many things to learn. These began at the armory counter when the rifle's metal stuck to my palms for the first time. They continued as I raced around the yard and held it close, as I laid it next to me in bed and learned to recover it as I woke, before opening my eyes to anything else. They continued with our drills, instruction in moving between standing, kneeling, prone shooting positions, molding muscle memory so the body could do these while the eyes kept steady down the sight, maintaining vision over what mattered. It was down at the range that these lessons took the next step, our squad arriving down the hill after the one before it had begun, and I tried to give the appearance that my ears were not rattled by the explosions going off from the far side of the concrete wall. They gave us earplugs, showed us to insert them to protect ourselves, reminded us to align the iron rectangle, exhale, and shoot down the middle. Then they took us inside the wall and tidied us in a row in prone, staring down our sights at the cardboard men twenty-five meters beyond.

My rifle's hour hand clicked from SAFE to SEMI, 9 to 12 o'clock, a new season under heaven. I held my tiny rectangle against my target's cardboard heart and squeezed. A quiver in my breath at the moment of compression, forcing my bullet high and wide. I winced at the recoil, retreated to SAFE o'clock, and came now to be aware of a presence over me. It was Shimon. I was embarrassed that he had seen, and yet reassured that he was there. Without taking my eye from the sight, I listened as he stood over me:

"Before you fire, take two breaths. The first breath is for your enemy. The second breath is for you."

A code, like Chaim's, a natural law. I would adopt this one, too, and I looked again through my sight to apply it. But as I began to draw my first, I stopped, because it was backwards.

First for the enemy, then for me—he had to have meant it the other way. I pulled my eye from the sight to ask, but he was already gone, standing high over the next trainee down the line. I returned to my rectangle and the man beyond, to 12 o'clock, and decided despite myself to accept these words of Shimon's as I had his others. I took a breath for the cutout in front of me, and was on mark, a second breath for myself, and was still. I squeezed, and though a cardboard man makes no sound, no cry when pierced, I felt my second bullet strike right through the heart where it had been aimed.

The mood changed in our last few days at Michve Alon, because we were all going to make it: every mother country, villains and cheerleaders, ignorants and scholars, we had earned our stamps and would be assigned to combat roles, serve alongside natives, begin basic training the very next week. Friday, they held a commencement for us on the great yard where we first arrived. Upon signal we tossed our berets to the sky like mortarboards, now graduates of this proving. These olive drab berets, though, they were no real honor: they were the mark of a newbie, a soldier yet to earn the distinctive colored beret of the unit in which he served. But still we flung them high, because we were soldiers nonetheless.

We were free of Uri now, and as we left the yard, there he stood barking at a noncom like he would never dare at Shimon, who stood away from it and watched our exit instead. There were things I wished to say to Shimon, but it was not the time and I had not the right. In Israel's army of brothers, "breaking distance" is a revered ritual: when the time comes in a soldier's training, the formal distance between him and his commander is abolished. The soldier no longer needs his commander's permission to speak, is forgiven his obligation to stand and salute. Commander and soldier now go by first name, share stories and fears and first cigarettes. The hierarchy between them, of course, remains, the commander's influence not diminished—on the contrary, through intimacy, enhanced.

But there would be no distance broken here at Michve Alon; it was a privilege earned in months, not days. Too great a seismic shift for our compressed time here, too much a cheapening of the rite to be earned with our real commanders over months to come. So I looked back at Shimon where he stood on the yard, and I had never said a word to him without being spoken to first, but now gave a silent thanks as we slung our kitbags onto the parting bus.

Our bus journeyed back south to Bakum, three weeks older than the one that left its gates for Michve Alon. We were all the way in it now, the grand circus: the Bakum that every Israeli, born or made, passed through on his way to basic training. Our tributary had joined the river, where the current was fast. This circus had more than one tent, and we animals set up shop underneath them, preparing to spend the night and tomorrow be assigned to our brigades. We awoke at sunrise to wait in lines through noon, each soldier a list of stations to hit, chief among them the placement interview in a small room with the silver-pinned officer, the Sorting Hat to decide your lot and stamp it in bright ink for you.

My assignment: the Nachal Infantry Brigade, the first preference I had stated on my written form and the one I voiced across this table to the waiting Hat. My rehearsed justification, two vocabulary registers above my real one: that Nachal had a proud history of closeness to the land, and of accepting foreign soldiers and valuing their contributions. That I found great beauty in the brigade's slogan, *HaYitaron HaAnoshi*, "The Human Advantage," which was true, except that I left out the part where I also found this to be an extravagantly presumptuous advantage for anyone to lay claim to.

My papers stamped in the colors I sought, I grabbed my belongings from under the circus tent, now onward to join my clan, to where the others waited for transport to our new home at Nachal's flagship base in the Negev. It was there, seeking shelter in the same shade, that I made friends with my first platoonmate. Dror was a fat Ethiopian with a nihilistic ease in his every breath. Eighteen years old, he had gone into conscription not kicking and screaming but laughing instead, and saw no shred of evidence that any of this deserved his serious consideration. I found him sitting in the shade shooting spitballs at the flanks of officers storming by, and decided to have a seat against the wall beside him and see if he had anything to say to me.

There was not anything yet, not while we sat baking together against the wall, but I was sure his heart rate brought mine down by proxy. And when the bus arrived and we rose for it, he sat next to me in the aisle. He asked why I was here, and as he spoke no English, I did my best in cobbled Hebrew, my story coming forth purer now that I was forced to tell it with a preschooler's sophistication, stumbling over the story as unartfully as our old bus over the coarse gravel. I searched for the words to unfold to him the truth, and he listened mostly in disbelief, his feeding my own while our wheels rolled us out to the empty desert. And yet this disbelief produced not anxiety but ease, a coming down from the fear of being without answers, a comfort toward being a spitball soldier, the first time since donning this uniform that I turned around and laughed at it.

When we arrived on base, I stuck at Dror's side the same way at Michve I had sought the middle—because I had a sense I was safe with him. And the guys adored him, because he was vulgar, irrepressible, and impossible not to root for. Our commanders' reprimands only emboldened him, gave him more to laugh at, left them steaming hotter air. He would fart in response to being called out by name, roll around like Thud Butt from *Hook* as accouterments to his push-ups, us his adoring Lost Boys. He took his thumps with a grin and a song, a martyr we had not asked for, but one we needed. The officers dreamed, I am sure, of stringing him up by his testicles on the center flagpole, even if they knew he would have found a way to put that joke on them, too.

But Dror never made it to the flagpole, because they called off the arms race and dropped him from combat before end of first week. After trying most everything else, the only way they could make an example of him in front of us was to make him disappear altogether. Dror would land in a noncombat role, a *job* in loanword army Hebrew. Spend three years stamping papers or changing tires someplace his insolence would result in missed deadlines and not lost lives. Wherever they took him, he would not be too hung up over it. The rest of us were, though—death is hardest on the living. *Dror*, as I remembered to look up later in the pocket Hebrew-English dictionary I had packed from home, was a literary word meaning "freedom." And freedom had other places to be.

Before he left us, Dror was a final frolic with what we all mourned. Dror's failing was not in his courage—he had more of it than any of us, perhaps more of it, too, than those ranking uniforms in whose general direction he farted. Dror's failing was in his spitting refusal to be unfree. Because fitness to be a soldier requires not just courage, but bondage. In my twenty-two free years, it had not yet occurred to me how all my life I had off-loaded my unfreedoms to soldiers in uniform as I off-loaded my soiled laundry at the cleaner's. And so went Dror, and I thanked him for the dance.

But it was in this same week, before Dror left us, that my other angel came. Sam, as he introduced himself, or Shmuel as I came to know him, was an American like me. Born and raised in Maryland to a Messianic Jewish family, he had studied Greek classics at Vassar before making *aliyah* ("ascent"), a Diaspora Jew's move to Israel to gain citizenship and a home. For Shmuel, who wished to build a family and enjoy a lifetime here, there never was a question that his first chapter would be in uniform. His service was the discharge of an obligation: unlike me, he understood before enlistment this unfree burden that awaited him, and came forward to embrace it, having left all frivolity behind him in *galut* (exile).

Shmuel had a scar on his cheek, a mild one, just enough to touch it up with a valor it needed. I later learned from him he had gotten it in a childhood hockey accident, but still I continued to imagine he had sprouted it solemnly upon arriving in Israel to pick up a rifle. His Hebrew was stronger than mine, in part because his Hebrew exam had come out the right way and he was given three proper months at Michve Alon. Like me, he was enamored of this language's innate poetry and liked speaking in higher register, and so we learned beautiful words together, using those where we could and English otherwise. His brother Zach was my friend from Brown, a tie we did not discover till the third week, hunched over a canned tuna brunch in the field talking about the people we had left behind. But it made sense. Shmuel and Zach had the same eyes, and these eyes had the same way of fastening their gaze an inch above you and into the clouds beyond, after you had said something that mattered to them, something to give their consideration.

This, of course, was the consideration Dror would fart your way instead. And Shmuel seemed Dror's pure contradiction, the two friends who would despise one another, two angel-demons whispering warring words in each ear. And it was true I wished to be more like Shmuel, who I sensed would be a stellar soldier, and true, too, that Dror was a garbage soldier, a fatality of week one—yet his chaotic laughing avatar was with me also. I knew Dror was having a better time of it, and that he had an honor of his own, and I could not forsake him, either. For now I contented myself to think that if they took us to war, I would want all three of us in the foxhole, two angels over me, a free press, so that when it mattered most, neither one of them would blind me to the other.

12.

In a later time I would read a poem stating in simple terms that freedom is nothing but the distance between the hunter and his prey. I had read this poem before: it was the story of these first days in uniform, my blended dreams and waking, my running always running. Because in these days I was beginning to forget my running count of the times I had felt something like a soldier, which had to mean I was becoming one. Sunrise in the tents, my own nightly running interrupted by the wake-up call, I passed the baton to my wristwatch so that it could start running as soon as I had stopped: five minutes to shave before presenting our clean chins for inspection in the yard. To the bathroom, where we faced ourselves in the narrow strip of mirror that ran above the sinks along the wall. In this clouded mirror stood the hunter, just seconds ago done running in his dreams, now staring back through one eye with the second still shuttered, shivering in this uniform, four minutes and thirty seconds to go, consummately unfree. Or was it that this shivering was a writhing at the clouded image of this armed hunter coming for me, at the knowledge he was drawing closer and closer until he would catch me, until he was no longer out in front of me but already inside. In the way that a free gazelle steps upon a hunter's trap, then writhes within it while the hunter is still at some distance, the thrashing animal depleting itself as the hunter approaches, the broken gazelle limp and expended by the time the hunter has swallowed up this separation, this freedom, this distance between hunter and prey.

The day the hunter caught me in his trap was the day I

got the answer to whether I would be able to go on this way, go on running. End of first week, the squad out baking in the yard in an accidental lull between commandments. Our bodies and wristwatches sitting at zero, their sloth a heartrending sin to the eyes of the master sergeant who happened upon us. Now, the two great metal ammunition shelves that housed the rows of tactical vests we would learn to wear, they were determined to be sitting on the wrong side of the yard. These shelves, tall as any of us privates and long as two, had urgently to be repositioned to the far side of the yard, from which such shelves would cast their shade in a less obtrusive direction. Three minutes for the task and now in motion all the bodies in the yard, save for the highest-ranking body, which stood in the center at calm. Twelve of us to one shelf, enough to hoist it with a grunt and hurry it white-knuckled across the yard, steel toes kicking heels, setting it down with care. The master sergeant's reminder that what remained to us were a shelf and a minute-thirty. We dozen sprinting back, another common grunt and the second shelf on its way under the sun, bare fingers twitching, grips failing, the sergeant's courtesy ten-second bellow, these ten not enough for the luxury of caution, one end down, the second crashing through our palms to the concrete, boots flying backward, a blunt force trauma clean through the toe of the one boot that did not quite escape: mine.

I had so far been faithful to the mandate to speak only Hebrew on the yard, but now my Anglo-Saxon obscenity echoed back from the base's far concrete walls. An open question whether a right big toe remained to me, hopping on my left as my mates looked on, their watch timers blinking at a pathetic zero.

"*Ta'amod kmo sh'tzarich* (Stand properly)," and the master sergeant approached.

I stood properly before he commanded me to be carried up

the hill to the medical tent, where my yowls had summoned the medic outside. Two mates threw me on the table in the tent, and when I opened both eyes on the medic, he winked as he untied my laces. "I heard you down there. That better be the only English we hear for the rest of training."

I snarled and watched him pull back my sock to reveal a mess beneath, too much spouting blood to yet see its source, which toes, what was still there. He frowned, I threw back my neck as he wiped me with searing alcohol, I took another look down the table, finding the wound at the end of my big toe, in the form of a red line thick as the edge of the shelf that had stamped it there at an angle nearly square, slanted just enough to remind comfortingly of the randomness of fate. The toenail's tip was pulped at the point of impact, its base wrenched clean out of its bed and into the air by the same force, white ribbons dangling, the whole apparatus like a destroyed seesaw. At the sight of it, I stopped thrashing, and like a trapped gazelle I laid my neck down—today there would be no more running.

The X-ray at the army hospital confirmed the good news: it was an avulsion fracture, a shearing off of the tip of my bone at the point of impact. The shelf would have done the same obliteration, the doctor explained, wherever it had struck: it was a heavy shelf.

I nodded in the evaluation room.

But in this case, he went on in gently accented English, it was a modest shearing, from which I would recover by absorbing the chipped piece and regrowing in its place. An undisplaced fracture and the bone's main mass intact, I would need no surgery, only a splint and crutches, and in six weeks I could expect to run as I had before. He congratulated me on my good fortune, because my injury's mildness did not reflect any heroic bone density on my part, but just that the shelf had fancied falling where it had, and not four millimeters farther.

"It is the way we speak of bullet wounds, too," he added for context on my way out the door.

Back on base, I would be placed on *bet*, the letter signifying not just the second-class uniform but a second-class soldier, an injured one who remains on base in a limited role. As a *bet*, I would spend the next weeks now lame in addition to deaf and dumb, stripped of the physical ability on which my dignity had rested, no longer even a strong idiot, my squadmates breaking formation to run, and I in their trail, limping far behind.

On occasion they would leave me altogether, gone to the field for drills or marches, myself behind to clean the kitchen or the yard. It was one such morning, for now alone in the quiet yard, given a trash bag and told to have it spotless before their afternoon return, that the wind picked up and the sand followed. Once it started, it came, and I had not seen a desert sandstorm before but became sure that was what this was, the far side of the yard already obscured in the wind, my black bag billowing violently, its contents spilling across the concrete like garbage tumbleweeds, our great army tents coming loose at the stakes and the sand lashing their undersides, our flimsy cots huddling for cover beneath. I stood alone in wonder and, having nothing else to do, began to limp against the wind in an effort to recover my fallen garbage, fearful of what they might otherwise do to me upon return. And so I walked, dark clouds swirling all around, never once farther from Kansas, before I tripped my broken toe over a tent's exposed iron stake and went flying, propelled an extra yard by a timely gust of desert wind.

There I lay facedown on the concrete, bag flown away and gone forever, broken toe throbbing as the sand closed in—and I froze, as a playing child does after colliding with the concrete, in the instant before it occurs to him to cry. I thought of Amy, my ex-girlfriend, whom I thought I had loved, the only person who never could get over the idiocy of my decision, or at least the only one to say so to me straight. Amy, with whom it had all been rather wonderful, whom I had broken up with on a splendid autumn afternoon in Providence, who had started med school at Penn while I journeyed off in quest of ever-farther sandblasted circles of hell.

But I did not cry. Instead I rolled over on my back to face the sky, did away with the pretense of sheltering myself from it. Uncovered my face, the fevered sand raking across, and there was Shmuel on my first shoulder, shielding his eyes, unable to bring himself to look on; Dror on my far shoulder cackling madly, eyes bulging with glee, fat body rolling around in the wind. I laughed with him now, Dror and I, howling together into the gale, the two of us convinced that the whole price of admission had been justified by this gift alone, this cleansing mortification of the flesh, this ancient microdermabrasion of the Levant.

13.

Strength snuffed out, I reinvested in scholarship, and where I limped, my pocket dictionary followed, stuffed in the back of my fatigues. My love for Hebrew blossomed because it was this language of drill-yard poetry, the code that migrated first through my viscera and then senses, before my brain. Long before approaching fluency, I held phrases that made hollowed gray shells out of the English way to say the same thing, because for me, these phrases were charged with the memory of what I had expended to learn them, where I was when they landed and stuck.

Hebrew words are based in *shoreshim* ("roots"), stems of typically three letters, manipulated in patterns to mold nouns, adjectives, verbs. The principle is that the *shoresh* contains an essential nature, manifested in new forms through each word grown from this common source. An outcome of the *shoresh* system is that two words meaning quite different things may be understood as far branches of the same tree, nourished by the same root. These threads would not reveal themselves when I first learned a word but only sometime after I already held it, hearing it said the right way to smack me awake that this word and another, despite different faces, were obvious twins.

The noun *shalom*, "peace," stems from the same *shoresh* as the adjective *shalem*, "whole." A simple parallel, and yet through it we learn more of both peace and wholeness, even though we knew both words before. Likewise, even though I had known the words *neshama*, "soul," and *linshom*, "to breathe," I learned more of each one as we sat in our first marksmanship class on essentials of breathing. The connection came alight, and in the same moment was so obvious it baffled me I had not seen it before. I remembered Shimon then, and I had not thought of him since Michve Alon, but I smiled now to recall his image, and wondered where he was.

I emptied my lungs for the second time—for myself—and squeezed. The cardboard offered nothing in response, no sound, not even a flap in the wind, though it had been pierced through the core. Taped crudely on the cardboard was a paper printout, a grid of black lines inviting me to fire at its center, then to replicate that shot best as I could, five shots in a tight cluster. The dream, to thread the last four bullets all through the same cut as the first, like there had only ever been one.

Success was measured only after the fifth shot, by the distance between the two bullet holes falling farthest apart on the grid. Four tight shots and a fifth that fled was a failing mark: each of the five required steady succession, each one to remember the one that came before. And here I had nothing to remember but the shot I had just fired, sheltered from the sun where we lay in a row under the roof of the range. It was silent here apart from our weapons' steady explosions, which beyond our earplugs were comforting white noise, the nature sounds undergirding our meditation. Our prone positions were intended to provide the most points of contact with the ground, the greatest stability and fewest variables; beyond the iron rectangle just one immobile target, just one job. My toe ached, but here it was no handicap: I could lie still as long as I desired, collect myself from the recoil, prepare to fire again after two new breaths.

The first day they took us to the range, my mark was best in the platoon. My squad commander, Tal, made sure to let the rest of the squad know. They looked at me as they had not before: lost and stumbling boy still staring at the sand, who had dispatched today's cardboard with unmatched precision. I felt their looks linger, ones I wanted back again, and felt a warmth rise, too, toward the rifle slung on my back. The next day at the range my mark was best in the company, made up of my platoon and two others. It had not surprised me when they posted the marks, because I had known these five rounds as I fired them, had tied each one to the last, not discharged any one until it was time. And when we would return from the range to the yard, and I again limped behind as they marched uphill, back to the hard place where strange words flew and healthy legs ran and I stood alone, I would long to return to the range.

And so the safest place on base was the one of live fire, where I continued to light up the cardboard, every day at or near the top of the chart. I grew a fast gratitude not just to my rifle but to Shimon, under whose natural law I learned. In the first breath I found my target. In the second I found stillness, and ease. He was right, of course, about their order—and this second breath seemed his secret, when I watched the others fire after a single exhalation finding their target, assuming redundant a second one to find anything else.

I thought of telling the secret of this second breath, but there were reasons not to. I treasured having one hidden leg up in this place that gave me no others at all. And I was afraid, not of sharing my treasure but of losing it altogether, exposing it as make-believe. Having my gift laughed off on delivery and being asked where I learned such nonsense, being made to shoot on one breath, discovering my marks were the same. Because like a great many natural laws, mine was a bit nervous about the truth.

So I guarded it. And my pride began to rebound, the company's most helpless soldier shooting like one of its best. And though I shot well because it was solace, I shot well also because we were being watched. In these first weeks each soldier was evaluated for several specialized roles. Among them, two soldiers would be assigned to the MAG machine gun and a third to the Negev light machine gun; these roles required great athleticism and endurance. Others would be designated team commanders to lead subgroups in combat drills; these were selected for early leadership exhibition. And to each squad two sharpshooters: the designated marksman, a hybrid sniper-infantryman wielding a specialized rifle to enhance the squad's precision and reach of fire. These, selected for their promise at the range.

Within our company were platoons 1, 2, and 3, and in each platoon a squad *aleph*, *bet*, and *gimel*. Nine squads, nine great tents in a square adjacent to the yard. My squad, 2-*bet,* held the landlocked second tent in the second row, center stage for the sound bleed between the surrounding eight. At night our ears were privy to these surrounding provinces' scuffles and songs, and often we supported them in chorus—our privilege and our charge in the heartland of this squalid federation. And one night in early winter, the hoots and hollers from 3-*bet* of the northern lands alerted us they had gotten important tidings.

The company's squad commanders, each on his own timetable, had begun revealing to their soldiers the roles they would carry. Adam from Philly had come a ways from being my fellow Bakum trash collector and was now a 3-*aleph* team commander. It suited him: he was unflappable, and among our company's several Americans, it seemed only he had emerged at the head of a squad instead of huddled within. Avinoam, another American, would hold the primary role on 1-*bet*'s MAG; this made sense, too, because he was an extraordinary athlete who routinely threw men on his shoulders when their own legs failed. I learned then from Shmuel, in neighboring 2-*gimel*, that he had been named a sharpshooter. I had grown accustomed to seeing his name near mine atop the charts: he was obsessively disciplined, and his fire as measured as his words.

As these names trickled across the yard, 2-*bet*'s commander

Tal had still not revealed our roles, and our tent buzzed at night over whose names would be called. Others floated my name for sharpshooter, but I insisted on not hearing them, because sharpshooter was a role of prestige, more than a cardboard sniper. Where he went, the special rifle he carried was a social proof, a signal he had been chosen as a protector. When the tent chatter quieted for sleep, it was replaced by my own, spelling out to myself that of course I would not be a sharpshooter, that I shot well but was a burden otherwise, that the only place I could stand on my own feet was where they were not beneath me at all but in prone, splayed out to the side. My toe was nearly healed and I would soon resume training without restriction, but I had spent our formative weeks a cripple, so many indignities that my eyes stayed fixed to the ground beneath their weight.

By this time I had broken from my limp and resumed a careful walk, but other habits remained. The next evening, I drew a late guard shift at the post overlooking the front gates, at the far end of base from our company yard. It was dark when I set out, and though I was able to walk now, I had left myself a thirty-minute cushion to limp across base. But once away from the yard and no one watching if I stumbled, I decided to break into a full stride. My toe was stiff but it struck the ground and my other foot followed. I strode longer, and then the first time in weeks two feet had seen the air together at once. I put two hands on my rifle, back and forth across my chest, a full run the rest of the way, huffing and puffing up to the tower twenty minutes early for my shift, the guard now at alarm, spooked by my race to his tower at a time nothing else appeared under attack.

"Why are you doing this?" he shouted down the ladder, with more unrest than he had had occasion for in the four hours past.

"I lost track of the time." This satisfied or at least quieted him, and I climbed the rungs into the tower before letting him down (we knew the rules: never an empty tower), without further exchange. He set off under the lights in the direction of the yard, and when he was gone, I settled into my aloneness watching the gates.

It was an hour afterward that another soldier appeared below making his way toward me. It was Tal, who came to the tower and called to me he was coming up. He began to climb and I thought I knew why he had come, but kept my eyes on the gates now firmer than ever, for these seconds he spent on the rungs.

"Good evening." He stood up next to me, smacking the coat of dust from his hands.

"Good evening, Commander."

"In your case, I wanted to inform you in private that I have chosen you to become a sharpshooter."

Into the open air that I left between us, he added, "*Kol hakavod* (Well done)," and turned to go.

I welled up with tremors that turned to thoughts that might have come to words to then form questions, but he was already climbing back down the ladder and bound for the yard, his figure casting a growing shadow down the concrete from the white lights on the gates. I stood back and held my hands to the tower rail, unable to fathom I would need to spend these next three hours without a soul to tell. Unable to funnel any part of this flooding river to another, I kept all of it within me, all of what he had just given, and with it I looked down on the glistening gates and the dark beyond, seeing them both in a light more vivid than ever before.

14.

Slow exhalation brings about a natural reduction in heart rate and an up-cycle of the parasympathetic nervous system, producing clarity of vision, restfulness, calm. The sympathetic nervous system's survival mechanisms, brought to the fore by rapid inhalation, are downregulated as unthreatened lungs empty themselves, bringing momentary quiet before the next drawn breath. Lying here in the dead of night with my newly outfitted M4A1 carbine, absorbed in the green sand painted by my Lior infrared scope, I felt my heartbeat slow at the end of a long breath out, in the openness before the next. Finger off the trigger, unpressed for time because no one was watching, counting. Across the range trained intently through his Lior was Shmuel; the lone Americans, this no longer our first name anyway in this tribe. I emptied my lungs again, still no finger on the trigger, and here I was at last a true graduate of Michve Alon, the gray crucible where we had arrived from the world's four corners sharing only our otherness, every man an other for his own reason. Now a dozen prone men without a world beyond the one in the scope, our mother countries were the squads we came from, and what we shared was that each of them had chosen us, for the same reason.

I gazed out at the iron cutouts which stood in a row beyond, protruding from the green landscape, the head and shoulders of an enemy unknowing that from three football fields away in the night, he was seen. Then like popcorn cooking, we began to fire, and this was a different game than the cardboard grids had given us: this one rich with instant gratification, as each strike to the iron man set off a shower of brilliant sparks into the night sky. Then a wait for the speed of sound to bring the second prize, the hard metallic pang back to our ears, completing the cycle. For a while I lay and admired the fireworks my men were putting up, just us, us boys, together lighting up a carnival of golden sparks in the night.

I prepared to fire on my man, returning my finger to the trigger and measuring my crosshairs just a proper nudge above his head, to account for my bullet's arc from here to there. After two breaths, I squeezed, and now remarked for the first time that three hundred meters became none, sparks soaring, before my finger was done following through on the trigger. Then I heard my metal pang, and resumed breathing long and slow, and aimed the second of the twenty I carried.

It was number ten or twelve when I aimed, exhaled twice, and squeezed only for my finger to hit a wall, a stuck trigger. A *maatzor*, a jam. One funny thing about jams is that they occur as a bullet is fired, due to the failure to feed the next round— yet you likely do not notice until you aim and squeeze again, meeting with a frozen trigger at what may be a time you were sure you did not want one.

I was unpressed for time yet pulled my eye from the scope with the reflexive urgency that had been entrained in me, and rotated my rifle to assess the jam.

On Friday, February 25, 1994, Baruch Goldstein, a Brooklyn-born physician and army reserve officer with the rank of captain, woke up at home in Kiryat Arba, a settlement on a hill above the city of Hebron. It was Purim, a holiday of resilience of the Jewish people against those who would endanger them, a day layered in the symbolism of triumph and redemption. Baruch visited the mikvah baths to ritually purify himself, donned his officer's uniform, and descended with his Galil rifle to the Cave of the Patriarchs, within the heart of the city below. The cave is a site of worship sacred to both Jews and Muslims, who shared it tensely, congregating in its two separate halls of Abraham and Isaac. On this Purim morning it was also the time of Ramadan, and hundreds of Muslims had gathered in worship in the Hall of Isaac, Abraham's only son.

Baruch entered Isaac's hall with the resolute air of an officer fulfilling his charge. He was familiar with the practice of these worshippers before him, and he bided his time at the rear of the hall until the part of prayer where they prostrated themselves to the God of Abraham, their heads to the floor. He drew his Galil, advanced its hour hand to automatic, and from where he stood behind these prostrate rows, opened fire. The unarmed men and boys rising in terror, Baruch loosing automatic fire into their bodies, drenching their blood upon the carpets, steadfast as they screamed and stampeded. As he depleted his magazines, he reached for more, reloading and maintaining his tide of fire, until he squeezed his trigger yet again to find his finger upon a stone wall. With the reflexive urgency that had been entrained in him, he rotated his rifle to assess the jam.

It was a *Maatzor Baruch*.

That, of course, was an anachronism, because it had not yet been so named. Not until after this day, in its commemoration—and his. But Baruch understood: this shell wedged in its entirety at a cruel diagonal within the chamber, this whole failure to eject, leviathan of all jams. Baruch cried in anguish that the Lord would stay his hand; cried in rage and began to slam his rifle on the earth to dislodge the jam, before the brothers awoke to the lull in his fire, a group swarming him in unison. Though accounts vary, it is said they began to bludgeon him with, appropriately, a fire extinguisher, and that it continued to fall until what remained of him could be identified only by the dog tag that came to rest on the earth beside his boots. The official count on this Purim holiday was one hundred twenty-five wounded and twenty-nine murdered, as well as the death of Baruch, whose name meant "blessed."

On February 24, 1994, ten time zones to the west of Baruch, as he was awakening in Kiryat Arba on Friday morning, it was simultaneously Thursday sundown in Santa Barbara, California. I was five years old and I had been looking forward to this night, our congregation's Purim megillah reading. I held the gragger I had crafted at home for the occasion: the ritual noisemaker used to drown out the name of Haman, enemy of the Jews, each time it is read. As the cantor read the scroll aloud, I listened only for that name. And when it came, my gragger rose high and I shook it with vigor, over and over, as would soon be shaken the extinguisher in the cave, again and again, in this grieving triumph or triumphant grief, to erase the memory of one's enemy. And after we had together erased Haman, we laid down our weapons, and drank wine and played music, until we would come to face our next enemy, perhaps as Baruch was now arriving at the cave of our fathers.

I did not learn that day of Baruch's name. Not until seventeen winters later, starting tonight, looking down to find this strange and ugly jam. Even a well-maintained rifle suffers occasional jams, and for a soldier these must be matters of supreme intimacy, practiced to unconscious competence, till the hands know to move without waiting for the mind. There is the *maatzor rishon* ("first jam"), a simple jam occurring when the magazine is not seated properly to feed the next round to the chamber. The *rishon* is cleared by giving a whack to the magazine's bottom to reseat it, so that the charging handle can be drawn and a new round loaded. The *maatzor sheni* ("second jam") is more ornery: the bolt fails to seal after a round is fired, either because the magazine failed to feed the next round squarely to the chamber, or the shell of the just-fired round failed to eject, stuck partially inside. In either case, the *sheni* must be cleared by pulling the magazine, drawing the handle twice to clear the chamber, and reinserting the magazine to load the rifle anew.

But then there was this other jam, a rare mutation of the *sheni* in which this shell never had a chance at flight, crushed by the surging bolt at a violent diagonal, locking up the bolt and charging handle, the entire apparatus *fakakt* (Yiddish, "fucked"). To begin to heal from this crisis requires some force, some finesse, and some time. And tonight, looking down to see this abomination for the first time, rifle choking itself on a withered shell within, I sensed I was above my pay grade. From where I lay, I waved over the instructor, who viewed it with a smirk and called over the others to show them what I had accomplished.

"He has a *Maatzor Baruch*," the expert instructor explained to us. He borrowed my rifle and showed it to the others, who craned their necks to see while I lay defenseless on the ground below. Then he set about coaxing the brutalized shell out of my weapon over the next minute, before handing it back to me fresh.

A learning moment.

Because as I would learn, it was not just that the army jargon had adopted this commemorative name for the jam, and not just this instructor who would speak this name with an odd decency. Not only he who would repeat the name *Baruch* with a vague courtesy or ambivalence, with something less than unequivocal denouncement of this traitor to the uniform he wore into the cave, something short of an abject grief at the incalculable harm he had single-handedly sown to the fragile seed of peace.

"I admire his devotion, but not his act," Shai, my squad's square-jawed playboy and its other sharpshooter, clarified to me on a later evening. Shai was a fast squad favorite, for his credible after-dark tales of past sexual feats and his poise amid the trials of basic. He cemented his standing with the sharpshooter designation he had earned well at the range, where he shot with a reckless ease and turned in stellar marks in spite of it.

Shai was a cool kid, maybe our coolest. But as he said these words, I was stuck trying to imagine a cool kid from home saying of a Klan lynching that he admired the devotion, just not the act. Stuck wanting to ask Shai if he could admire the devotion of an Intifada suicide bomber, if not the act. I wanted to tell him he was making an impossible distinction, that admiring the devotion aloud meant admiring the act in quiet. I wanted to tell him this distinction of his was serving only to conceal from him his own hatred, to permit it to poison him from the hiding place he had constructed for it. But I had not the Hebrew to say this to him with grace, and I did not merely want his friendship, I needed it. And in any case, I was not in uniform to play the role of peacemaker, so I held my own peace, even though Baruch would not soon give me his.

In the wake of the Cave of the Patriarchs Massacre, Prime Minister Yitzhak Rabin said of Baruch, "I am shamed over the disgrace imposed upon us by a degenerate murderer." Rabin, who would be assassinated the next year by Jewish extremist Yigal Amir in the streets of Tel Aviv, denounced Baruch and those who would support him: "You are not part of the community of Israel."

"You are an errant weed," pronounced Rabin to the late Baruch, in his own final year. "Sensible Judaism spits you out."

But there were also those who would tell you they admired both Baruch's devotion and his act, at least achieving an ethical consistency in doing so. Baruch's rain-drenched funeral in Kiryat Arba drew about one thousand mourners, among them

Yigal Amir. "Everything he did was for the sake of Heaven," one friend eulogized, in reference to the revered text *Pirkei Avot*, the Ethics of the Fathers. Engraved into Baruch's tombstone is the teaching that Baruch "gave his life for the Jewish people, its Torah and its land." In a last pious gesture borrowed from the Book of Job, the epitaph adds of Baruch, "He was blameless and upright."

Baruch's grave sits in a green park above Hebron, a dignified memorial overlooking the cave in perpetuity. Upon his tomb rests an accumulated trove of stones, which Jews place on an honored grave in lieu of flowers, for their lastingness, their eternity. Baruch's specter alive and suspended over the city below, shrieks and gunfire still embedded in the cave's walls—not because his ghost must endure forever but because it is nourished by the living who gather in remembrance of his name.

After all, this was not a man gone mad, but one who followed through—and these people loved Baruch and all he stood for. Before descending on the cave, Baruch was an esteemed doctor, and though he refused to treat any Arab who came to his table, among his own people he was a dedicated healer who spurned prestige and financial reward. For Baruch, to heal his brothers and to kill their Muslim enemies stemmed from the same one *shoresh*: there never was a contradiction in preserving lifeblood and spilling it with the same hands. Nine days before Purim of 1994, Baruch was interviewed for a documentary, he an object of fascination, and was asked how he reconciled his charity with his violence. He responded unflinchingly with the voice of Ecclesiastes: "A time to kill, and a time to heal."

PART II

15.

Spring came to the Negev, and I became a son in a new home. This *bayit* (home), of all the flying words on the yard, was from what I could tell most sacred of all. Although the soldier loves his country, *bayit* is not that, not the homeland he stands on but the home he left to get there. And because the homeland is small, no matter what desolate hole he finds himself in, he may comfort himself that *bayit* is not all too far. He will have the luxury of a fair amount of *bayit* during his service, and spend much of the rest of it longing for more.

Out in the field, the thought of *bayit* recalled to him two treasures: the mother he would find there and the sergeant he would not. *Ba'bayit* (at home), he is pampered in slow pleasures and remembered liberties, free of the cling of his uniform and of all accountability but the kind he chooses. *Bayit* forms the core of his morale, and his rationed doses of it are essential to his training: his sergeant respects *bayit* as the counterpart to his own lessons, knows that *bayit* does not draw the soldier away from service but renews and sculpts him for it, that *bayit* is the restful night in which he assimilates what he has learned by day, and which reminds him—more than any sergeant could—of what he trains for.

And so the great task that separates the foreigner from the Sabra, the native-born Israeli, is not the former's acquisition of language or of culture but of *bayit*. Santa Barbara was my birthplace but it could not be *bayit*. Nor could Eli's—his hospitality would not expire, but I would need to find *bayit* elsewhere, if not for Eli's ease, then for my own.

A soldier without family in Israel is termed *chayal boded*, "lone soldier," a dignified pejorative that affirmed my condition only a short time before coming to enforce it instead. A lone soldier could also become a strong or respected one, but these inessential names could not sneak between "lone" and "soldier" where they fused, could not subvert his nature, which was to bear *boded* (lone) in a place his squad's other eleven were not even aware they bore nothing at all. And so I came to find that "lone" stood in the way of the other kinds of soldier I wished to be, and thought that even if I could not erase it, I might forget it, by finding *bayit*.

So in pursuit of home, which was the pursuit of not being "lone," in my first weeks I had put out a call for adoption, floating a sparse bio through the army's adoptive-family program so that an earnest family might come across my thumbnail and decide I was their boy. It was in the spring, a few months after submitting my ad and long after forgetting what I wrote in it, that it came to be answered. A family on Kibbutz Be'eri, a prosperous kibbutz in the Negev, had chosen me. Like Eli's, their acceptance had been whole and sight unseen: they made clear I needed only to decide whether to accept them back. When I learned they wanted me, unconditionally, it left no question I wanted them, too—but still I was given a special half day to travel across the desert, to meet this family and decide if they were mine.

Be'eri, whose name means "my well," sits at the northwest edge of the Negev just a few miles from the Gazan border. It dates from 1946, in the special company of kibbutzim predating independence, and though it stands on sovereign Israeli land, its proximity to the border has brought it under the shadow of rockets fired from Gaza into the homes and fields of Israel's south. I had not yet been near the border and it daunted me to think I would live there, but then again this was to be *bayit*, my well, the one I drank from and the reason I fought.

There is in the Negev a fleeting season, at the end of winter and the cusp of spring, in which the desert erupts into red bloom. These *kalaniot* (red anemones) are drawn forth by winter's cool and rain, and they overtake the landscape, engulfing it in a mesmerizing scarlet. Because the *kalaniot* will stay only a short time before ebbing into the hills under the heat of spring, many Israelis flock south to be awed by them before they go: in particular to the western Negev, along the Gazan border, where the conditions bring the *kalaniot* to grow richest and fullest. I had not before known of the *kalaniot*, so on my bus westward across the desert, toward *bayit*, I sat alone at the window and watched these dunes breathe in red. I had no name for this wonder and needed none, instead discovering for the first time the way the hills bled deeper and more gorgeous red as I continued to draw nearer the border.

I thought about meeting Izzy, the father of my new family and the only one whose name I had so far been given. It was a blessing he had not answered my call for adoption till now, for in this time of waiting, my broken toe had healed, my Hebrew had taken leaps and bounds, and a sharpshooter's M4A1 now rested on my lap. Eli had housed me as an infant, performed my *upsherin*, sheltered me in my regression—and yet I was glad Izzy would not meet that limping infant; that he would meet something closer to a man, one who would step off the bus and look him in the eye as we shook hands, as a father and a grown son might.

And I found him there on the open green, past the yellow guarded gate at the entrance to the kibbutz, into where rolled the fields and flowers and the graveled paths. He waited there and he knew who I was, because he had seen my adoption mug shot and now saw the way I came, armed and in uniform but looking for home. As I walked to my father but before we shook hands or said a word, he glanced down at the weapon I carried, my M4A1 with its scope and bipod. He did not comment, but I knew what he knew—and I felt a swell of pride in my jaw as he welcomed me, and as he turned to lead the way to the home where Noga, his wife and my mother, waited for us.

She had baked a plate of cookies for me, her second act of unconditional love. Her third was to wave to me from the front doorway, hug me and say they had been longing to meet me, and hoped I would accept to stay. She did not know I had accepted them before I got on the bus, accepted them again as it rolled past the beds of throbbing red hills, and accepted them once more as Izzy smiled on the field, all before I had found her, calling and waving from under the doorway of home.

On Friday two weeks later, I came back through the yellow gate into Be'eri as a resident for the first time. Today I would also meet Izzy and Noga's three children: my sister Paz of ten years; brother Arad, eight; and littlest sister Dotan, six, who would all soon be coming home from school. For now, mother, father, and son sat in the shade outside and ate ripe oranges from the kibbutz's orchards, and I began to learn from them of Be'eri, of her work at its laundry center and his as groundskeeper of its petting zoo down the way. Be'eri was a wonderful place to live, they affirmed. Unlike many kibbutzim, it had been able to remain near to its original socialist vision, and its resources were owned by its members and shared by them according to need. Vital work like theirs was no less or more than the roles others filled, to meet the community's needs. Due to Be'eri's size and resources, it was a cultural center in this rural region, and its amphitheater was a frequent stop for musicians or speakers touring the area. It had about a thousand residents, which was large for a kibbutz, but small enough that there were no strangers. The children were free to leave and play in the morning and come home in the afternoon, and they locked no doors on the houses that did not belong to them anyway. Be'eri had, really, everything it needed, and certainly everything that they did.

I sat and listened, and these were impossibly sweet bursting oranges, and I was on my third when my three siblings arrived home in a sudden row, one after the other, each of them lighting up and running with the things they carried, down the path to come meet me.

Arad was first home, stocky and bright-eyed, and I stood to hug him as he bolted toward me. We paused to set down our things, I my rifle and he the crayon drawings he had brought from class, so that he could jump into my arms without obstruction. I remembered then the rule that I was not ever to set down my rifle while away from base unless securing it behind two locks, so I put its strap back on my shoulder as Arad showed me what he had drawn.

Paz came next quietly with her backpack. She came to hug me, and paid an attention to my rifle that Arad had not, stood back with a new look brimming with questions. We sat and she started strong, asking why I was here. I was again glad to have grown my Hebrew before arriving: whether or not my family knew any English, Hebrew was what they spoke, so it was what I would speak with them. I had not been asked this question in some time, and this one was easier than the same one Dror had asked on the bus—easier to locate Hebrew words, easier to know which ones I wanted. She had asked why I was here, not what brought me here: reasons, not causes, which meant my answer was not limited to things I knew before arriving. I began with Santa Barbara, where I was born. Then I had started trying to spell out reasons, and to name the people behind them, when another person appeared on the path: my third sibling.

Dotan was last, and carried nothing. A strikingly pretty little girl whose blue eyes sparkled in the daylight and blond braids flowed behind her as she ran, and jumped high into my arms for her first hello. Instead of coming back down from our hug, she climbed farther, swung around onto my shoulders, and planted herself in seated position. She took hold of scraps of my buzzed hair at the sides of my head and began to nudge them left, right, and forward, to direct my movement for her joyride, my guided tour.

And so we took off, Dotan and I. And I waved to the others and said we would be back; Izzy and Noga laughing at the two of us. They did not seem troubled that my M4A1—the one Izzy had known instantly—still hung low, unloaded, SAFE, from a leather strap on which their daughter's legs rested. Dotan, who sat at the helm making machine sounds while I trod beneath her weight, gave no hint of trouble either.

"*Kadima* (Forward)!" And we were off down the path, Dotan pointing left and right, naming the houses of friends we passed, the gardens, the *cheder ochel* (communal dining hall), the playground before it. This was where my function changed, because she dismounted to run to the swing and called for a big push. I gave her one and then another, and it was between these pushes, standing on the sand while she held on and flew, that came my first spare moment to collect all that had welled up within me in the hour since arriving through the yellow gate.

"*T'nadned oti* (Push me)!" I gave her another push, and she laughed and flew again, higher than before. The sunlight had grown orange around us, and I had not thought how long we had been there. But I remembered I was hungry when she said we should go get ready for Shabbat dinner. She began to lead us back toward the house, pausing first along the way to name a new stop on the tour.

"Do you know *Tzeva Adom?*"

I did; I was familiar with this term. Red Color. Despite its plain name, it referred not to a color but to mortal danger: it was the name given to the automatic alarm system of Be'eri and other communities in the region that came under the shadow of rocket attacks from Gaza. Qassam, Grad, Katyusha, and other rockets, of varying range and capacity, all of them incapable of precision, all of them fired for precisely this reason. Fired for this unstable lethality, so that neither prey nor hunter could tell you where was safe and where was death; fired for the way those two thus began to blend boundaries, for the way this crude rocket's deathliness was not contained but leaked, crop-dusting tiny bits of death as it flew. Fired by a hunter aiming less to kill his prey than keep it bounding wide-eyed forever; fired for the violence the rocket inflicted while still soaring high in the air, spreading its black and growing shadow on the earth below.

And so upon detection of a fired rocket, this alarm fired on loudspeakers gripping the kibbutz, sufficient to jar you from sleep or where else you may have drifted. No shrill siren, no earsplitting horn—instead, in one recorded female voice, *Red Color*, words a six-year-old knew. She called four times, and though she kept one calm tone throughout, her first call was a warning and her last a proclamation punctuated by explosion: *Tzeva Adom* (and time to drop everything and run, sheltering time varying by location), *Tzeva Adom* (but in the case of Be'eri so near the border, about fifteen seconds), *Tzeva Adom* (screams filling the space between her words), *Tzeva Adom*, impact.

"Yes, I know of it."

"Good, you know, if you are at the playground when you

hear it, you run to this shelter and leave your things behind no matter what."

She had stopped and pointed again, and I had not noticed what we walked past as we left the playground—but it was a concrete shelter, a red sign at its entrance. I stopped now, too, there with her as she pointed at the bold red letters on the shelter and waited for me to read.

And yet, the color red, I remembered as I stared into the letters, had been my favorite for as long as I could remember. I had loved red since I was her age, or even younger.

Colorfully anointed stalls lined the sides of Santa Barbara's downtown State Street, and all the world glowed. I was five years old on a summer day in 1993, and my beloved mother tugged me through the Sunday farmer's market in a Radio Flyer red wooden wagon. I carried nothing, not even my own weight, as our wheels hopped and rattled over the pavement, adding punctuation to the sensory treats all around. At the center of my world, my mother's sundress gleamed in the daylight as she held the wagon's long handle and towed me through. She turned her neck back to check on me and, for a lasting instant, smiled down her arm at me where I sat in the wagon. When she turned back to look farther down the street, my favorite market stall came into view ahead.

The strawberry man's sign was printed in vivid red, its letters made of fire-engine red strawberries and their dancing stems. I called out with delight.

"Mommy, can we get strawberries?" When she looked back to me, I was already holding out my finger, pointing at the bold red letters on the sign.

"Of course we can. Pick your favorite basket."

My mother helped me out of the wagon and I rushed to

the stall to find the brightest, most overflowing basket on offer. She had only just handed a bill to the berry man as I chomped into the first berry, releasing a mess of red juice onto my shirt. I climbed back into my red wagon, holding close my basket and its treasures, and I put the basket in my lap and grabbed a second plump red berry, chomping into it as my other hand reached for a third. As I ate, I saw my mother look back down her arm to me and send another smile, then turn back ahead and continue pulling me along, our wheels again rattling toward what other wonders the market might have in store for us.

"*Hakol b'seder* (Is everything okay)?"

I must have drifted before reaching the end of the sign, because I looked down and was surprised to find Dotan there, her finger still held out, pointing to the shelter. The alarm had first been called *Shachar Adom* (Red Dawn) until the name was changed to avoid unfair association with Shachar, a common name for little boys and girls both. Shachar had been spared, but not red, not the Red Color, which, as the calm voice reminded four times on repeated occasion, was the very cruelest color.

"Yes, it is good to know that, thank you."

"Here," she said, perhaps unconvinced, stretching out the same little hand toward me. "I will hold your hand on the way back."

I gave her my hand and she took it, my left palm open forward and her right sealed over it, and she led us along the way home. The orange sun behind us, we walked toward our shadows, thrown longer down the path than when we had set out. Though her hand was locked over mine, protecting it, you could not see it in our two shadows, which were instead linked at the arms as one, her long braids swaying at the edge of her half of our shadow and my rifle's barrel at the edge of mine. I looked down my arm to her as she hummed, and I recalled I was around her age when I decided my favorite color was red. Then again, I had never known a Red Color, only the color red.

I thought of asking what her favorite color was, but decided it was not the time. Instead, for comfort, I gave her hand a little squeeze. Then I felt her recommit, returning it to me.

16.

"*Amidah* (Standing)!" I leapt to my feet and snapped my rifle into position, staring down its sight at my enemy.

On *Yom Rishon*, I had carried back to base the image of Dotan, pointing at the shelter, trying to make sure I understood—and when I stepped off the bus, I found an extra breath in the first run our sergeant Ziv ordered on the yard. Now Ziv had ordered me to this duel against Viran, nimble team commander of 2-*gimel*, and so far I was winning. Our two squads encircled us in a dusty cockfighting ring, the two of us training our empty barrels on one another a few paces apart, springing and rolling and reloading as Ziv shouted orders, the others surrounding and egging us on. The duel's winner would be the first man to arrive in position and shout *aish* (fire) one complete movement ahead of his adversary. Till then we seesawed, Ziv shouting the next move and the two of us scrambling hands before mind to execute.

"*Shkivah* (Prone)!" Fists to the ground as our legs flew out behind us, eyes down our sights before chests hit the dirt, targeting one another as our ears strained for the next call. "*Gilgul* (Roll)!" Jerked my rifle to my chest and propelled myself clockwise over the earth, landing after 360 degrees, finding my crosshairs in the dust and now Viran within. I was half a move ahead of him. "*Gilgul!*" Again the world upside down, still spinning at the edges as Viran rose to center. "*Maatzor rishon!*" Smacked my empty magazine and drew the handle, staring back down it when "*Maatzor sheni!*" and my magazine caught a clump of dirt as I yanked it out over the earth, slammed it back into the holder, but it would not click in, I pulled it again blind, eye down the sight where it needed to be, shook the magazine and slammed it but it would not click, and "*Amidah!*" and Ziv would not have called that if Viran had not already cleared his jam and I looked to my magazine to clear the clump stuck on its edge and "*Aish!*"

Dead. Fallen champion of 2-*bet*. Viran's barrel bore down on me triumphant from where he stood as 2-*gimel* cheered and my men dropped their heads.

"Benjamin, you are dead," narrated Ziv. "How are the fruits of *Gan Eden* (heaven)?" I kept mute because I was dead and knew my place. Ziv turned to my survivors. "You have a dead soldier, what do you do with him?" He motioned only his head across the way back to where we had made camp, two hands steady on his rifle, signaling it was time to carry the fallen home from the field.

My boys appointed Glazer, our broad-shouldered MAG gunner, to carry me over the dunes. They took my weapon as I had no longer need of it, and another man swapped his M16 for Glazer's MAG, because Glazer was permitted to take a lighter weapon so long as he never went without one. Glazer rolled me over face-up and then laid the back of his head on my belly, his arm underneath my thigh so that as he held me and rolled onto one knee, my body would fall into place across his shoulders. As he took hold and rolled forward, I felt myself heaved into the air, and I raised my arm to grip his shirt and hold on.

"You are moving a lot for a dead man, Binyamin," came Ziv's remark from the earthly plane. I went limp, and Glazer did the holding, beginning to carry me up and down over the dunes for what seemed a far greater length than camp had ever been. He strained beneath me, stopped and panted, heaved me about on his shoulders, kept up his heavy steps. My uniform had ridden up and my bare hip collected sweat from his jaw where they pressed together, my neck dangling limp off his side, center of gravity creeping over the edge, body threatening to tumble, impulse to hold on tight, the way a dead soldier could not. I was falling, but he would not let me. So I let go, and kept limp as he panted, lifeless as he shook, and I moved not a muscle but to shut both eyes to the world (surely a dead man was allowed that much), placing all my trust in him to carry me home.

17.

For a warrior, it is always personal. So Ziv had stated, offhand, about a month back. Another natural law like Chaim's or Shimon's, though unlike theirs, I had not felt prepared to adopt Ziv's at the time. I decided anyway to keep it around, and in time it came to be the one I held nearest.

It was the law I held on our first run last week, after Dotan had showed me the shelter. And the one I held today as our company met at Yad Vashem, Israel's Holocaust memorial, and walked its halls with berets on our shoulders and heavy red boots on our feet. And the one I held on a frigid winter day about a year later, after release, when I visited Auschwitz in the same boots and left the tour group to walk alone, to place their tracks there across the central yard.

When my *bubbe* was imprisoned in Auschwitz as a young woman, she would see the birds singing in the open sky above, and they would fill her with envy, and also with hope. And after liberation, after coming to America with my *zayde*, starting a family, and reaching the day that she had all the bread she wished to eat, she has loved to take pieces of her bread, and feed the birds.

On this morning, we finished winding through the halls and emerged to a beautiful day in the hills of Jerusalem, and they gave us the packaged deli sandwiches we would often get on outings like these, and sat us at the picnic tables outside. Though some chatter started up, I found myself sitting with nothing to say, except to take bits of bread from my sandwich and toss them to the pigeons that had gathered nearby.

"How was it?"

Noam was another sharpshooter. Squad 1-*gimel*. I had not even known his name until we began sharpshooter training and were spending all our days and nights together at the range—but he was fluent in English, and once he sat with me to translate a lesson I had not understood, and then we were speaking English all the time, despite the fact that neither of us was supposed to.

Noam was rarely first to speak, but these words were an invitation. He meant them. Before speaking, he had sat down next to me, opened his sandwich, and joined in tossing bread to the birds.

"My grandmother was in Auschwitz. Today she still has the stamp on her wrist."

"My grandmother, too, was in Auschwitz." He did not hesitate to respond. "She and my grandfather met in a displaced persons camp after the war, decided right away to marry, and came here to be part of the new country in 1948."

I looked at Noam, sitting beside me tall and lean with his sharp uniform and red boots and M4A1 in his lap, and had the jolt of staring at a mirror in a place unexpected, the nakedness that comes with being just the same.

"My grandparents also met in a DP camp. They were engaged, then had to decide where to go. He wanted to start over in Israel. But she won out, and wanted to come to America instead. She said that for one life she had seen enough war."

18.

The M4A1 inspires in its holder a kind of inferiority complex. He carries something exquisite, a system with few or no remaining faults in its performance of the function for which it is conceived. Such a faultless system has a fast way of laying bare the defects of its user, almost as if by design.

A fine example of a "mature technology," the sum of decades and billions in minute advancements over predecessors that were already, truly, quite good. The Vietnam M16 was a very good technology, the M4A1 only a little better. If there is any fruit left on the tree's high branches, I never saw it—though at Colt Firearms in Hartford, Connecticut, they are still looking.

Before the marksman becomes any good with the M4A1, first comes his discovery that he is only striving, to the extent possible, not to be its limiting factor. There are many ways for him to ruin its effective function, so he begins by addressing the easy ones: he learns shooting positions, and within them to master his posture, arms, fingers, to subordinate them to the rifle, to extinguish their contrary impulses.

From prone, his aim is extremely stable, chest and arms on the ground and rifle's fore on the bipod. He cannot now escape seeing the way his breath tugs the crosshairs up and back down, maddeningly over and under, a disruptive and ceaseless tide. He grows averse to it, an obstruction, a frailty, to be subdued like all the others.

An unnatural thing, this, to detest one's own breath and wish it defeated. But he wishes to be a marksman, and so before long, he will breathe as never before: inaudibly, uncommonly, and remorsefully.

It had been another morning like the others, sinking into our marksman's lungs of our own accord under a dispassionate sky. There was the clear lens and the iron man within, and nothing without save the occasional flick of a bullet casing on one's shoulder, exploded from the chamber of the next man down the line. True randomness, it seemed, was the trajectory of a scorching ejected casing. Once, while lying prone, Shmuel took one through his *bet* uniform's armpit gap and into his shirt just under the left nipple. From the far side of the range, I had the sure impression someone had been shot. He was able to get it out of him and stop howling but only after most of its heat had dissipated into his flesh in the shape of a standard 5.56mm SS109 casing, and I understand the skin came to regrow, but not the follicles, which were claimed that day by the Negev.

But those odds were remote, nothing to lose focus over. There was nothing but the iron man, and now from the adjacent range the faint rippling bursts of the Negev machine gunners unleashing torrents upon their own iron men between bear crawls over the dunes. As I quieted my lungs on the head of my iron man, I could scarcely abide the thought of such bestiality in our world. Here was discipline. Here was harmony. Here was order.

"*La'asof tarmilim.*" I was pulled back to the earth by the command from over my shoulder: Pick up the shells. All of them.

The shell is the heavy part of the bullet, one whose weight is carried throughout the bullet's life, though it is perceived as a separate component only after. It is the same part that gives the bullet its vigor, without which it would have none, would be only an inert little ball. In our long ecstatic fusillades we would not take notice of our shells until made to, at what then seemed the surprising rate of one hollowed shell per round, piled on all sides of us and long gone cold. In our hours of shooting we were spared this distraction, and the commander kept silent until just these two words, *la'asof tarmilim*, at a time we had forgotten they were coming. Then the sober clicking of rifles to SAFE and the quiet gathering of our mountains of shells before exiting the range, before returning and forgetting again.

We left the range like new, then sat for mealtime on the slope outside before resuming for the afternoon. I made my sandwich and looked for Noam to continue our talk from breakfast, but did not see him, even though all morning he was shooting right beside me on the line.

I remember of Noam that he seemed tired of being eighteen. He did not slip into the contagious giddiness of the rest of us in our long volleys on the line, and seemed the only one to take even longer than me to fire. He helped me master the adjustment of the crosshairs for the ballistic arc: just above the iron man's head, because at three hundred meters the bullet is already on the downside of the arc. He sat with me during that lesson so I would not get lost, and I learned it in his clear English, which he swore he knew only because he had loved Hollywood movies from a very young age. Otherwise we spoke mainly of before the army, in English, which was a favor to him because he wanted to learn to think in English, too, he explained. He had a special love for Tim Burton films, and at breakfast we were discussing scenes of *Big Fish* and I was still there because I had not spoken in the hours since, and I had more to say to him but he was not here.

So far that was fine, because he might have gone off behind a dune to take a dump during the free time, but when we wrapped and stood again for orders, he was not in the row.

They sent a couple men out to look for him while the rest of us went back inside the range.

It was a bit later they called us, all the company together, not to stand for orders but to have a seat and listen. Noam of squad 1-*gimel* had gone missing earlier today, started the company commander. He paced a bit as he got going, and I came to find it easier dropping my eyes from him to the ground below his feet instead.

Noam had set down his rifle behind him and wandered a couple hills over, somewhere far enough to be alone but close enough he would probably be found. There he had sat down and slashed both wrists with his Leatherman army knife, his other weapon, the one with ten or more functions, the one he had not used in a while.

I stared at the cracked earth.

The men found Noam sitting there alone, peaceful in his eyes, his open wrists taking turns spitting blood onto the sand. He had folded his knife and put it back in place.

These tiny grooves woven in the dry earth, my eyes traced their edges, not about to glance anywhere they might find others looking back.

They rushed to bandage him, hauled him back to base, and stopped his bleeding. He was going to be okay. They put him in a clean uniform, gathered his journal and things, and his squad would have a man watch over him until he was on a bus out. He would be reassigned to a noncombat role, and it was important for us to know he would be fine.

The commander seemed unprepared for the silence after he was done, which persisted until he told us all to rise. Coming now to my feet, eyes staying low to the earth, to the cracks we stood on.

Then we got going, and that evening Noam was not beside me on the firing line. Soon came the command to gather our empty shells, and then our line rotated out to switch from the daytime Trijicon scope to the nighttime Lior. We stopped for dinner outside, and as we broke bread, it hit me this was the second meal in a row Noam had missed.

"Maybe he didn't like what he saw in his scope," Shai offered to break the silence, munching on his sandwich, then asking for a mustard packet passed his way. He slit open the packet with his Leatherman knife and pasted more mustard onto his white bread.

"Just above the head," I heard Noam repeat to me a moment later, as I positioned my Lior on the iron man in the dark. "At three hundred, the bullet is already falling in the arc."

19.

I thought of Noam's rifle, with which he rarely missed, alone in the sand where he'd cast it.

We did not talk much about him after he was gone, which gave me the sense his loss was with us all the more. Dror, whose name meant "freedom," had left us a while ago now, and Noam, whose name meant "gentleness," had made it some time longer before removing himself, too. We grieved the both of them, yet the difference was that Dror-of-blessed-memory remained the stuff of campfire tales and reenactments, while Noam had four unspoken walls around his name. This was not just because our commanders had seemed to set those walls for us, nor just because Noam, unlike Dror, had been a valued, humble soldier——that is, one whose fall was harder to explain. More than these, we were telling one another with chosen words and chosen silence that what we lost with Dror we would remember loudly, proudly, while what we lost with Noam was a harder thing to say.

What was sure was that Noam had chosen to go, surely as Dror before him. In a manner, the fact he was alive and somewhere out there made him harder to bring up, because it meant the one unique place we could know he would never be again was with us. He left behind a hollowness, and in his wake came new disorientation and doubt, severe as in our earliest days of training, when Dror prepared to leave us first.

Feeling more exposed than we had since week one, it was good they had begun now to have us train in body armor, harder shells in a time of need. Armor we would not earlier have desired, not before spending these months studying how soft we were beneath. And if at one end of the spectrum of penetrability was defenseless *bet* and at the other invincible *aleph* (not available in the field), we had progressed by now to wearing the in-betweens.

First came the *shachpatz*, the flak jacket that afforded moderate protection from shrapnel, knife slashes, and other external hazards. It was an older technology and these were vintage pieces with dried discolorations one did not ask about; and the best of them had sharp jutting collars and rows of pockets that made you look like a Gulf War commando. The *shachpatz* would not stop a bullet but was an intermediate shell, and a prelude to the rigid *kerami* ballistic vests we would wear later, once we came to have need of them.

I was headed now to my shift at the base's western boundary, a post for two, which made a long night shift a refreshingly different exercise, an intimate conversation in the dark with another voice than one's own. My partner Nagosa and I striding west toward the sunset in our stained *shachpatzim*, I took advantage already of his presence by speaking out loud, which on solo shifts I would not commonly do. I feel like a turtle in this new shell, I said in the way of a prayer, not because Nagosa had any answer but because he would hear. What are these even for, I lamented, it is not like they will save us from bullets anyway. Nagosa was a pace ahead and did not respond, so I began rhetorically repeating to be sure he heard, when he spun around with the Leatherman knife he had been nonrhetorically opening, planting its blade in my core.

I looked down, the knife's handle sticking out of me springing up and down like a cartoon diving board. Bringing my hands to the stab in a perceived slow motion, to receive the thick pooling red that would appear on them, the mortal wound announcing itself beneath, my eyes' dawning understanding, their peaceful fall, which was the way this would go.

"You see?"

And I saw. Because Nagosa's voice came like an angel's, arriving at once with my realization there was no wound. My dense *shachpatz* had halted the knife cold, spitting it back to the sand.

"Have you fucking lost it?" The mortal wound had left me now, and with it its peacefulness.

But he seemed the sounder now of both of us as he bent to retrieve the blade for its next use, and assured me he had tested it against his own vest already, which was how he knew. I could not remain angry at him, his knifing not a test but a demonstration that my vest had held me safe all along. It had already been a more revelatory conversation than I could have had on a solo shift, but we had not even reached our post so we got moving in a hurry to avoid being late to relieve the two who waited for us. A capital affront to a soldier, worse than merely asking him the wrong question.

"*Yesh choter* (Is there a twig)?" This was the right question. Really, the only one.

The *choter*, though so called, was not in fact a twig. It was the artifact of our common cleanliness ritual, the rifle-cleaning rod anointed with oil and driven through the barrel to remove its impurities. Without regular cleansing, a man's rifle grows fouled with the desert's filth, prone to lock up and suffer horrific jams, like the one whose name I learned on the first night with my M4A1 at the range. A dark night of the soul, because a rightful stigma attaches. Because a soldier who keeps an unclean rifle is worse than professionally negligent, is in a state of spiritual ruin. So we cleaned of our own accord, habitually while the company's religious men gathered for morning prayer.

Today at sunrise a group assembled at the high point of the next dune, beyond our rows of tents in the long valley below. They donned the white shawls each kept in his field pack, faced north to Jerusalem, and cloaked themselves as color came to the sky. The sight was arresting, but aching, incomplete. If there were ten men, they would have a *minyan*, the quorum required for public prayer, and one would lead the service in call and response. But our company had sent just eight to the dune, no cantor, not one service but eight, the men congregated near one another but each one alone.

I watched Shapira, our squad's lone Orthodox, sway gently, silently, alone among seven others. And I wished to join, to complete, because there would be truth in that act alone—but still it would not be enough. I had to imagine if there were nine, one more of us would join. But not eight. To be the ninth required real belief. No one was going to be number nine.

"You want to join?" asked Barkan, noticing my gaze. "They always take converts."

Barkan was a *shpitz*, a stud soldier, from a secular kibbutz in the rural north. He came dark bronze, lean, and muscled from day one like he was on his second tour. An uncommon dignity, not reserved in his words but spare in them, not just undesirous of praise but contemptuous of it. Our squad's *MAG shtayim*, the second man assigned to the MAG, not the gunner but the support, who has more jobs. The one who hauls the spare barrels and heavy ropes of ammunition, keeps the gun healthy and slinging, though he trains to fire it, too, in case. The embodiment of *bet*, which until not long ago I'd have thought was an unkind thing to call someone.

"I'll go if you go, too."

"Not for me. I believe in God. That's why I'm here and not there."

"What?"

"You think I would want to go before God with an unclean rifle?"

No, I didn't, now that he asked.

"*Achi* (Brother)," he kept on in my silence, "prayer is how the doubtful try to convince themselves. The louder they pray, the more unsure."

I was unsteadied by the sense of it. I watched Shapira now sway in vigorous prayer, his shawl's white fringes tracing in the air behind.

"What makes you believe?"

"The world is more beautiful if you see God in it. Who do you think stopped Abraham? Who do you think stopped Baruch?"

Shapira had stopped swaying. In its stillness his shawl caught the full embrace of the sun as it rose over, bathing earth and sky in a soft gold. To my relief, Barkan did not press for an answer, content to sit with me and watch the warm sun on the backs of the worshippers awhile longer, an army of eight on a hill, before returning his eyes and hands to his immaculate barrel.

20.

Sderot (meaning "Boulevards"), Southern District, Israel, population roughly 20,000. The nearest town of any size to Be'eri, which also made it the nearest town of any size to Gaza. Around fifteen minutes, up rural Route 232, from Be'eri; alternatively fifteen seconds, as the missile flies, from the border. A distance not in meters but in seconds, which are, as concerns the prey, the better measure of the nearness of the hunter.

A sleepy city that no longer ever slept, Sderot was something of a postcard town for Qassam terror. Now, its namesake boulevards were lined with a new, thoroughly pragmatic feature: the *Tachanah Memugenet* ("Protected Station"), a bus-stop-missile-shelter whose perplexing double function was to facilitate passage and prevent it.

Today it was a scorching Friday afternoon, and I was passing through to catch the bus for the last leg home, down Route 232. As the sun blasted, I was glad to reach the shelter of the bus stop's concrete walls, two feet thick, with *Am Yisrael Chai* ("The Nation of Israel Lives") tagged in electric blue paint on one inside wall and a green fire-breathing dragon on the other. On its outside, the structure's sole official signage read *Tachanah Memugenet*, in giant red letters I could make out from at least a fifteen-second sprint away from it.

The light was graying on the little ant running in the fissure in the earth, as Shmuel and I began to hammer down our pup tent for the night. He had just returned from evening prayer, where they were again just short of nine.

"There was a *Tzeva Adom* in Sderot on Friday," I confided. "My first time."

"Was anyone hurt? Where were you?"

"Waiting for the bus."

Even a skilled atheist—like a child who has found too good a cranny in a round of hide-and-seek—cannot long keep his peace. Given time, he will poke his nose out, start to whistle.

So I found myself alone at the station in the desert afternoon, and after I had settled, I began to whistle, almost home. Beneath the heat haze twisting on the dunes, spring's last red *kalaniot* burned wild in the fields at the border and the hills beyond, and even as the call came, *Red Color*, they remained as they were, crowning red flames spreading over the hills, *Red Color*, calm, clear, and sweeping through the burning red fields, *Red Color*, without any source, and without appeal.

"What did you do? Were you alone?"

"I remember being frozen when the calls started. Staring out past the border, at all the red flowers in the fields. It was just me in the shelter until a Haredi man dove inside at the fourth call."

His stark white image on a tear in my direction with all the air of a man catastrophically late to make his bus. His body thrown against the concrete, *Red Color*, and into the whites of my eyes, *Hear O Israel, the Lord is Our God, the Lord is One.*

The same prayer Shmuel had just completed, the one a pious Jew repeats morning and night each day of his life, and then once more.

"Wow, he said the *Shema*? Did the rockets strike near you?"

"No, distant booms. But you can't watch the rockets land first and say your last words after. If you have something to say, fourth call is the last."

"And you had nothing to say?"

"No. What would I have said to him?"

At this he put his hammer down and set his eyes on the sky an inch above me, which told me more was on the way. The ant had made it out of the fissure and I finished hammering the stake into the same crack, so as not to work against the grain.

"Seems each one of you was terrified by the other," he proposed, still to the sky.

"Terrified."

"Maybe even more than by the rockets?"

"You might be right."

He hit the final stake on our thin green tent, and we remembered both to switch to the Lior for night before securing our provisions inside.

"And what happened after all the rockets fell?"

"He got off of me and we sat down awhile together. It turned out we were getting on the same bus."

21

The Abrahamic faiths have for millennia had a handle on the trick that it is easier to get a sex-starved man to kill. Yet when I found myself all alone in the night, standing guard against only the encroaching abyss, brain exploding into its expanse, sexual deprivation was not the torment of mine. Before Eve was pulled from his rib cage, could Adam have been sexually frustrated, or merely lonely? And if she were ever placed back in, would he forget the feeling?

It seemed so. Sex drive was an output from an input. This involuntary cause-and-effect machinery, like gunpowder through a barrel, had never been more evident than now, when there was no cause in all the Sahara. I came to suppose that any man shipwrecked on an island would, given time, become asexual. Said another way: a tree falling in a forest without an ear to hear it makes no sound, yet it is also true—and less often heard—that any ear is a deaf one if without a falling tree or buzzing bee for miles.

Devoid of any such matériel for a while, the churn of the machinery went quiet. Sex drive, in turn, had begun to abstract itself, drift up to heaven. An early graveyard shift, libido not dead but finding its way from the barren dunes to the rich black sky, never once feeling more Talmudic, it occurred to me at last how monks might be able to thrive. Sequestered from the unrelenting clutches of Eros, freed to cultivate their lust after the image of a different God. And no doubt there was in this a certain liberation, which for a time was painful, then less. After silence comes peace: this perhaps was what the monks were after, another thing they knew and I did not.

But there were other hardships in the watchtower—penuries of other kinds. By no accident, while the yard was harder for the body, for the spirit the tower was training's harsher trial. The premier guard post was the *shin gimel*, at the well-lit front gate where trucks would rumble in and out in the night, and in the worst case the infirmary was not far. There was the armory, also a sensible place to put a guard, where lights were lower and one was alone, but comforted in his firepower. There was also the range, where one had only one weapon and was reminded not of possessing firepower but using it, and where there were no lights at all.

The range was a strange place to post a night guard. It was outside the base's walls so there were none to watch, only the sand that yawned three hundred meters from start to finality. No valuables either, only the iron men who stood there riddled with the wounds of the day before. Often we were ordered to lug their bodies, heavy, to the ammunition sheds for the night, which I understood was to protect them from the Bedouins who might rescue them from their perdition and redeem them for iron. But sometimes they were left out overnight, too, and there was no tower at the range so one stood not above the iron men but among them, a harder kind of alone.

Alone like I had imagined Paul felt in *All Quiet on the Western Front* after stabbing Gerard, who fell into the trench with him, alone in the separation between the parts of himself that were leaving now with Gerard and the others that remained. There with Gerard, Paul spent hours rifling through dying Gerard's letters, reading them, feeding him, longing to revive Gerard as he went still, because Paul longed for those departing parts of himself to return, because without them, he felt alone.

It was why I felt alone after Dror and Noam left, longing for them to return, and why you felt more alone here at the range when the men were left out with you than when they were not. They were just iron men from three hundred meters, not a real man from no meters, but still it was easier to shoot them in the day than find them still there afterward, not moving, at night. I had just started my shift and did not know whether they were there tonight at three hundred in the black, but I flicked on my Lior to look, even though I was almost sure there was nothing to protect. All of them in a silent row looking back, protruding motionless from the sand, each one of whom I had shot with slow, full intention in the day, one breath for him, one for myself. And I flicked off my Lior again, a surer instinct toward protection now than I had known in the moment before.

22.

The moment after was quieter than the one before. Before, a calm and imperfect natural quiet on a Jerusalem spring afternoon. After, a shrill, perfect, man-made silence that did not follow the explosion so much as complete it, an organic part of the whole. The long tail aching noiselessly in the air, before the sirens began. After the child hits the concrete, before he begins to cry.

On March 23, 2011, I was spending my Purim holiday in Jerusalem, the first half with Eli in the hills and the second with Yoav from back home, who since summer, had been living here in the sunny district of Nachlaot. Yoav was both my nearest link to Santa Barbara and a veteran of my battalion, so I had leaned on him often in training, called him in the free evening hour we were given before bed, took his prized advice such as keeping Johnson's baby powder on hand for marches in the field.

It was great to be back on his balcony overlooking Nachlaot's bright alleys and synagogues, just steps from Machane Yehuda—but the air was drained now, and even before the sirens came, we started to move. I was wearing *aleph*, like I needed to be to ride free on the bus today back to Be'eri. And I was armed, carrying the sharpshooter's rifle that signaled I was one chosen as a protector. But as we hit the street and the sirens came wailing, I was smaller than unarmed Yoav, wanted him at my side, because he made me feel safe. And so we walked, Yoav and I, rifle hanging at my back instead of in my arms, toward where the sirens bled in the air, walked and not ran, the pace of a protector sure of little other than that he still wants permission to be afraid.

A bus bombing outside the central station, at the stop where I would wait for the bus to Eli's house back when it was home, the stop I got off at yesterday on my way from there to here. In this round there would be dozens injured and two dead. The first was fifty-five-year-old British national Mary Jean Gardner, a Christian translator of the Holy Scriptures. The second, by a long margin, was fourteen-year-old Hodaya Asulin, who suffered catastrophic brain damage and would remain in a coma until succumbing in 2017 at age twenty-one, though she had been murdered today, at fourteen.

It was not a suicide bomb but one placed and triggered from afar, so I came to wonder if he watched the news afterward, read about Hodaya like Paul did about Gerard, even though Gerard was a hostile combatant who left in an afternoon and Hodaya was a schoolgirl, who would take longer. Came to imagine him reading all he could find about her life while it slipped away and her birthdays passed in the bed, seven, before he was alone.

But today Yoav and I did not know any of this, only the silence that completed the blast, and the sirens that followed. And when we arrived, since we had walked and not run, there were already barricades up, so I did not cross, though over them I saw the blood soaked on the phone booth I liked to lean on while waiting for the bus. Dripping from the walls, shining in the full light of the sun. I watched from behind the barricades, parachuting slowly into fear, confusion, or anger, not yet landed, not yet knowing where I would. But there were others who had landed faster and harder, and a throng of Haredim now gathered over the shattered glass chanting "Death to Arabs."

Disperse, ordered the police, the first bomb could be bait to draw a crowd for a second one, but their rage grew denser and more ecstatic, so I kept a fair distance because it was an order. And I held my rifle now with both hands, because this was an order, too, my primary function since my first days on *aleph*, even though I had still not finished training for my function on *bet*.

And there were other soldiers on *aleph* like me, arrived before or after on the scene to take up their rifles with two hands. I watched us together, there behind the barricades while the paramedics shouted over the crowds and tended to the dying, comforting ourselves with our rifles' hard metal, fulfilling for our own sakes the only duty we knew how.

23

At the end of Be'eri—beyond the petting zoo, where its speckled goats and lambs roamed freely, yet before one came to its two outer walls of barbed wire and the German shepherds bound to patrol the corridor between them—there lay a great open field.

I found it early in my time, because it was the most peaceful place on the grounds, a large and untended expanse, its soil cracked and raw yet nourishing a scattered set of orange trees which dotted the field and lined its edges. With rare exception I would be alone there, and I would sit on the hill at the edge of the field, safe from alerts or imperatives, free from oppressive words or eyes, and far enough from the rifle I had secured behind two locks in my room at the far end of the grounds.

And on Shabbat, the day of rest, I would love to run sprints in the field. I would start from underneath the branches of one orange tree, and go until I reached the shade of another that marked the distant end of the field. Our commanders had urged us to continue exercising when home, and yet I ran not to obey but to defy them: I ran on the field in tennis shoes, to take higher strides than my boots would permit. To drain my lungs and make them suck in freer air, to have them seethe with this air, and to do it of my own will and no one else's. These were mutinous exercises, the least soldierly thing I ever did.

I preferred to go in late afternoon, once the earth had absorbed the heat of day and the light came soft. And there I would race back and forth in my open field, running till it was just enough, collapsing in a grateful heap upon the earth. I would heave out my air and draw in new, replenishing myself before rising to pluck ripe oranges from the trees. And then I would sit, perched on the hill at the field's eastern edge, and there enjoy the oranges, looking to the west as the sky grew purple around me.

On this evening, though, I sat on the eastern hill with Izzy, and the people of Be'eri teemed all around us. Tonight was Lag B'Omer, a minor Jewish holiday marking Day 33 of the Omer, the 49-day period between Passover and Shavuot, and a season of austerity and mourning. Tradition mandates restraint throughout the Omer, and forbids weddings, live music, and other indulgences until the redemptive day of Shavuot. Lag B'Omer is an anomaly within that season: a day on which the Omer's restrictions are lifted, and the people find renewal on an island of revelry and pride.

Though Lag B'Omer's origins were as a rabbinic holiday, it was reimagined as a Zionist one, owing to its association with Bar Kochba, last great rebel against the Roman occupiers of Judea. It was on Lag B'Omer of 1941 that the Haganah (the IDF's precursor, in the years before independence) established its elite strike force, the Palmach. Seven years later upon independence, the government order creating the Israel Defense Forces was issued on this day. The day carries a vindication of the Jewish fighting spirit; the day is resilience in the midst of the Omer's dark. And so although this day was only at the periphery of my American Jewish upbringing, it meant more for the secular people of Be'eri, who did not bother themselves with the Omer's restrictions anyway.

Tonight at sundown the people gathered on the field for an *al-ha-aish* ("on the fire," a barbeque), the air thick and sweet with meat on charcoal. Music flowed from concert speakers set up at the edge of the field, and at its center raged a mammoth bonfire, a teepee of great logs leaned onto one another and set alight, like the kind my Boy Scout friends once showed off with when we went camping, but of biblical stature. I felt the fire's heat warm the hairs on my shins even up here on the hill above, and now and then it would pop dramatically, wood shifting within it and the great fire sending a brilliant volley of sparks into the night.

My rifle was locked away back in my room, but now with a little jolt, my hands felt around me for it, because these flying sparks were just like the ones the iron men would give when we hit them in the dark from three hundred. I wondered if this, like the Hebrew coming into ever-sharper focus on the yard, was another force of nature that starts losing its wonder once you come to know it a little better.

I turned to Izzy, who sat beside me while we watched the fire, waiting for Noga to arrive before we went to join the feast, the three kids nearby sitting with their friends or playing in the field below. I had a question for which I had been hoping to get him alone.

"Do you ever think of leaving Be'eri for somewhere safer? For the sake of the children?"

It was a rude question the way it came out, a presumptuous one. But I had not realized it until it was through my lips—and it was in any case an earnest one, too, one whose answer I ached to know.

"*Ain l'an livro'ach m'zeh* (There is nowhere to run from this), Ben."

I was silent afterward, watching the logs twist and groan, the bonfire soaring skyward, an exquisite searing orange.

"You do not like the way the rifle sits on you."

I had not expected him to speak next—but then these were not new words; they were only the next words of the sentence he had already spoken.

"I am not sure."

"Did you expect to be sure?"

"Yes, I am almost certain I did."

"Why did you come here?" This one came without further delay, father like daughter. It was like Paz's question when she met me, though it seemed Paz had asked it for her own sake and Izzy now asked it for mine. And it was just us now, no Dotan humming down the path to save me. I thought of telling him I had done it to honor a friend who had passed. No. Izzy deserved a more honest answer, as did Avi.

"I'm no longer sure of that either."

We were silent awhile, the fire growing stronger still around the wood, letting loose a river of sparks for the sky. There down on the field was Arad, kicking around a soccer ball with a pack of other boys. He paused now and then to turn his back to the fire and wiggle his shoulders up and down, to soak them in its warmth. No accident, I thought, they built the Lag B'Omer fire here, at a distance from the nearest concrete shelter, in the great open field.

"Do you think Arad will serve in a combat unit?" This was a new question, asked as soon as it arose to me.

"When the time comes, I will let him decide."

I looked now from the field over at Izzy. His eyes rested on the bonfire, or on Arad and his friends below. My questions had not offended him, had brought him not a moment's deliberation concerning the answers which he lived, and which he had simply repeated in words now that he had been asked for them. Noga would be with us soon, and in any case the *al-ha-aish* would go late into the night with plenty of food for us all. I stood to stretch my legs, and to turn to warm my back against the fire. As I turned from the field, there coming our way was Noga, who waved brightly and quickened her pace to join us.

"Here comes Mom," I voiced to Izzy, and motioned my head in her direction for him to see. He came to his feet to kiss her as she arrived. And together the three of us walked toward where the others had gathered around the platters, the great fire behind us shooting orange rivers into the night, Arad safe with his friends in the field below.

24.

Late spring in the Negev brought our first fake war, and the second time they carried me home. *Shavua milchama* ("war week") was the crowning week of our advanced training: past the huddles on the yard, past the nights and days at the range emptying our magazines and the endless free refills, past the desert marches and the Bedouin guard dogs and the mornings waking up in two-man pup tents starting our reels with the cracks in the earth and the ants running through them. The 72-hour stretch of *shavua milchama* was all of these: one of our hell and Ziv's heaven, his charge to dutifully obliterate any remaining illusion of our control, we sleeping with one eye open and the second twitching, the plan never known till barked to us from somewhere we hadn't seen him, now a hill to conquer, a nested cast-iron sniper to dispatch, a fallen friend to carry. Before we set out from the yard, they did have us drop shoe polish in our 70-pound packs so that we could get a sheen on the boots in the mornings, appreciate a bit the worth of routine in times of trauma.

Because otherwise, these conditions were meant to do something like simulate those of a war. A sort of Lag B'Omer, where normal training regulations like a nightly seven-hour sleep minimum and three square meals were out the window, an exultant time of Ziv's freedom from those restrictions, an oasis of chaos and despair in the midst of order. And we were doing all the same things they had trained us to: these were the same crosshairs, same tuna rations, same tents we had slept in and taken down and covered with sand for camouflage in the dunes while we marched away for the day. If there was any difference, it was to make us come to feel like we did not know any of these things at all, that they were unfamiliar under the black cloud of fatigue, eyes clouded, regressing to the surest senses, such as the pitter-patter of the couple of lost ants racing down your thigh, searching for escape after they had taken a wrong turn in the pup tent this morning.

It was dawn of the second day and I was rooting for these kindred ants but too tired to help them, and we sat to breakfast, timers again racing as we pulled our premade tuna sandwiches from the plastic sacks in our field packs. More ants now, a stream of them on my plastic bag as I withdrew it, a thick and busy red rope of them woven through the bread, stings on my hand already as I pulled the first sandwich from the bag. I opened the sandwich and in another era I might have enthralled myself to wonder how long this great colony would take to consume its prize in full, but this morning I was angry, and I tossed the sandwich to the sand and then the whole bag, likewise long colonized.

I sat and stewed, drank water instead, and I accepted half of Barkan's sandwich but was still hungry when we rose. It was later that day between skirmishes, raiding our packs for another meal on the go to suit our active lifestyles, that I discovered there was no food in mine. I regretted tossing the bag, because I was sure I could have swiped off most of the ants and eaten, and anyway it was all I'd had, so how could I have decided that all I'd had was not enough. That night after another forced march and conquered hill, I got another half a sandwich from a friend, but my stomach ached when we went to sleep, and when they fired blanks in the air before dawn to scare us back awake, I was weak.

It was the final day and we would soon march back to base, where they would feed us like kings, but now both stomach and head were knotted and I wanted no feast, only to lie down. And soon we started our march, but my stomach curled into itself and rejected water also, and now the sun came violent, and its sky was blue and cloudless. I marched and I did not want to fail this test, this crowning week. But when I grew dizzy, I fell behind, and when I tried to catch up, I hit my knees. It was then that Ziv noticed.

"Are you all right?" He handed me a full canteen, and I waved it off, repulsed by the thought of adding its weight to my hands.

"I want to finish."

"You didn't answer the question."

At his order they heaved me into the air on a stretcher, a soldier at each of the four corners. They took my rifle, and now without it, I came to see how my head throbbed, vision swam, voices muddled in my ears. I was reassured to identify Oren, a lanky northerner who sang even in our cold showers, whose voice appeared from the stretcher's rear right handle, next to where my head had come to lie. Oren was rarely weighted down much by anything; now came his voice in a low and hard tone telling me I was going to be okay.

Ziv was shouting from somewhere far, and as they carried me over the rocks, my bed pitched and blue sky rattled up above, and where I lay, it all felt toweringly gentle. I was scared, afraid to lose consciousness. I tried to ask Oren something else but heard no answer, because either my words had not reached him or his lungs had none to spare. And so to keep awake, I listened to how his breath caught and shook as they stumbled over the rocks together. The midday sky was looking darker now, and I held my hand to the metal pole of the stretcher, and I do not know how long they carried me, except that Oren's labored breathing went on awhile, into the dark.

I was reassured to be lying down still, because were I not to make it inside heaven's gates, I imagined I would at least be shut out from them on my feet. Instead I lay, like I had on the stretcher, and all was gentle like before. But now it did not clash with a convulsing blue sky above; instead there was the calm beige of the 2-*bet* tent's canvas, the tent empty as I opened my eyes save for the medic over my right shoulder, who had replaced Oren there, given him a breather. I thought then of Oren and the unknown other three who had carried me, and though my first relief at being alive was a selfish one to know I had not been slain by red desert ants, my second was to know I would have the chance to find out who all four were, thank them, apologize for my idiocy. I must have then looked around for them again even after finding the tent empty, because the medic's first words were to tell me to keep still.

The guys were all at the mess hall enjoying the feast, explained the medic. I wondered what they were eating but had not the faintest interest in joining, my stomach still knotted into itself, crossing its arms in spite, spending its last vital saliva spitting at the world. But it was slowly being brought out of its tantrum, soft conquering hard, a gentle trickle to my bloodstream through the IV the medic had hooked to the inside of my elbow. I looked at the IV bag, and the medic, and was thankful for the both of them, too. I managed a *todah* ("thank you") to him, saw him nod, and did not say more for the next while, as the bag trickled and I enjoyed this most unique sensation of being irrigated, throat coating itself without drinking, limbs reanimating through this uplink with the angel who remained above my shoulder.

Despite my collapse I would be given credit for the week, because on our marches we had the practice of throwing a soldier onto a stretcher for the homestretch and carrying him the final way into the yard, then giving him three triumphant pumps in the air, the soldier skipping on the stretcher's surface at the top of the heave like a seated groom at his wedding. This felt off to me, because I was sure they had not done that with me when they kept rushing past the yard to the infirmary to cover me in ice sheets. And because I imagined this custom with the stretcher was to simulate saving a life, not actually do it, and that this week had been about the simulation of almost dying in war, not the near experience of dying away from one. But then I imagined I had learned from the week something like what they wanted me to—so I asked no questions, and the next night, after thirty-six hours resuming first fluids and then soft foods, they welcomed me back to formation.

It was a good lesson to carry to Har Herzl, Israel's premier military cemetery in Jerusalem, and the destination of our march the next week for the occasion of *Yom Yerushalayim*, "Jerusalem Day." I had twice now been carried home—once playing dead, once almost being it. And so as we marched overnight from the valley below Jerusalem, up to the city streets as the sun rose, up to Har Herzl as the honking cars drove by and cheered and waved blue-and-white flags out the windows, I kept whatever acquaintance I had acquired with the prospect of death, and prepared to enrich it further, which I imagined was why they had brought us here. Then we had arrived, after a grueling uphill march in which I stayed so hydrated, I was stopping to piss every ten minutes and running to catch up, a march to exhaust us, deplete us of armor and cynicism, bring us lower to the earth, closer to each letter carved on the gravestones before us.

And this visit was for us, given the morning after a sleepless night to roam the green mountain like a self-guided apartment tour. Living soldiers bringing themselves near dead ones, making ourselves less far from where they were, so that where they were would be a place less lonely, or at least less far, because after one is made to give up making death farther, what remains is to seek comfort in bringing it nearer. And so we visited the dead, now and in other days, at the graveyards and in the stories we shared, searing into ourselves images of commanders fallen on live grenades to save their squads, immigrant soldiers fallen oceans away from their waiting mothers, heartening one another with the promise that you, too, would be carried on your brothers' shoulders, the objective of the battle now shifted, your body now its most sacred spoil.

The cemetery rests on a gorgeous hill above the city, layered in pink tulips and unvarnished graves. All soldiers are buried side by side, regardless of rank or unit. Yonatan Netanyahu, hero of Entebbe, whose name inspires breathlessness four decades after his fall. Michael Levin, less a household name among Sabras but one of the first we foreigners learned about, an American fallen heroically against Hezbollah in the Second Lebanon War. These and so many others, their names neighborhood or national legends. The common thread, of course, was the word *nofel*, which means to fall, but is a hard translation. This is because in Hebrew, present-tense verbs are an anomaly: they are the same as the noun. In English, we have this sometimes (judge, judge; guard, guard), but in Hebrew it is the rule; it is the statement on the nature of things. You cannot judge without being a judge, nor guard without being a guard, nor fall without being a fallen. Because what a person does, now, at this moment, he is. Gone and redundant is the "-er" tacked on the end of the verb, because why ever pretend to escape from the identity of what it is that you do right now.

And so *nofel* means to fall, present tense, but also is the noun for a fallen soldier. In this case, of course, his present condition is his permanent one, is now his perpetual state. To fall forever. *L'olam* ("into eternity"). So I walked among them and was comforted to draw in near, but wanted less than ever to have any such story told of me, too. Because to be a *nofel* did not sound like rest to me.

25.

Never be in a hurry;
do everything quietly and in a calm spirit.
Do not lose your inner peace for anything
whatsoever, even if your whole world seems upset.
—Saint Francis de Sales,
1567–1622

My whole world seemed very upset. There is a certain way one views the world through squinted eyes, when he is squinting for at least a few reasons. There is the desert sun, which around this time late morning is high enough to scorch his skin and throat yet low enough for its blinding light to strike his eyes instead of harmlessly hitting the helmet jostling atop his head. There is the salty streaming stinging sweat, down his eyelids and into his vision, which he might wipe away were he not at full sprint clutching two hands to his rifle, back and forth across his chest, as he strides. There is his sense that, in squinting, narrowing his field of vision, he might through such reduction find a clearer sense in what left he sees, what other blearing part of the world there remains before him.

And I was not at war, of course. But these exercises were at least intended to bring us longing Pinocchios somewhat closer to that nirvana of being a real soldier, more so than all the other times we had lain in a row and pelted the iron men from a distance of three football fields in the dead of night, when we caught them by surprise, and then by surprise again, and again and again. These exercises involved the same immobile enemies, but at least now added the element of our own fatigue and confusion, our racing clocks and hearts, our sharp heaves of the lungs as we went to squeeze the trigger and until that involuntary gasp had been so very sure we had him.

And so I was, sucking wind through a rubber gas mask strapped to my face for the joint purpose of depleting my lungs faster, while reacquainting me with the image of chemical routes of death as well as ballistic ones. Crawling now or rather squirming upon the sand so that the iron snipers would not see me, keeping a low profile as it were, rifle to my chest while my elbows took turns jutting forward and my knees behind, in such a way as to make me question the wisdom of how we are told that a man begins and ends life on all fours, because I was sure this could not yet be the end, because after all I was, of course, not at war.

And sure enough, I had squirmed to the finish line as the percussion of fake war raged around me, it now being time to adopt a new worldview: a red crosshairs and strange surrounding constellations, arcane markings permitting a man ideal precision from wherever he may look, a worldview nothing if not adaptable. And this all left precious little time for reflection, stumbling now through the range's doorway, gripped now at the forearm by my commander and led to my shooting place, raising now my rifle to locate my man. And though my vest was weighty with ammunition, my magazine held just six rounds and I had only twenty more seconds to fire them, as if to suggest that, despite my full vest, I might not at war have the luxury of firing more. Two to fire from a standing position at the cardboard man at fifty meters, two from a kneeling position at the man at one hundred, and two last from prone at that iron man at three hundred, who by now, in light of all my commotion, I could scarcely believe was yet again being caught by surprise.

But it was the nearest man who threatened first, so I put my crosshairs on him, exhaled, and squeezed—but at the moment of release my lungs again heaved, forced my bullet to the sand at his feet. I found him again, steadied the red, and had him even as I pulled, redemption coursing to my finger and into the trigger—redemption halting there against a brick wall. Because again, one funny thing about jams is that they occur upon firing a bullet, but unless your spirit is calm and saintly and your whole world none too upset, you notice only on attempting to fire the next. Hands before mind, I rotated my rifle to identify the jam—*maatzor sheni*—and pulled the magazine to let the shell tumble, shoved the magazine back in, and redrew. I found my man again in red, came upon a stillness halfway through inhaling, and squeezed—but in resuming shooting position, I had not steadied well my rifle against my chest, and as I squeezed, it shook, just a nudge, my bullet now a nudge over his shoulder.

"Ten!"

My foe at fifty was alive and well and I doubted he would forgive two attempts on his life, but still I dropped to kneeling, butt on heel, rifle against my chest and firing elbow out firm to steady it against the wind, finding the second man, adjusted aim for distance, emptied lungs, and squeezed. But in kneeling, though one's vertical axis is steady—butt on heel, forward elbow on knee, rifle held tight—one's horizontal, the 3-to-9 o'clock, is known to wobble, a drawback compounded by heaving lungs, my red crosshairs now veering from his heart to the left one smidge, my shooting eye placed too close to the scope and absorbing a metal smack from its recoil.

My fourth flew in anger. I flung it in rage, willing my bullet to strike him not through the law of ballistics I had studied, but that of justice I had just decreed.

"Five!"

Two left and my legs flew out behind me as I dropped to prone, finding my man when a gunshot tore violent through my eardrum—because in dropping, I had caught the string of my earplug and yanked it from place, exposed now to the friendly fire of the next sharpshooter a few meters down, under a war of his own. Ears ringing, sight quaking, I found my enemy, squeezed, splitting my own ear again, gripping my rifle a second left now found him once more and pulled. My sixth and final shot producing no golden sparks.

Done, and I released my grip, resumed gasping, telling my bleeding ear it would be okay, it now becoming SAFE o'clock again on our rifles as out went our commander to count our marks. Mine, one out of six. The man at one hundred had, in fact, been pierced at the shoulder, a flesh wound, but a hit, so I had scored after all with my third. I knew this much, because it had not been my fourth, which lay gone and buried in the sand, distinguished from the thousands of others strewn around it, those forgotten, but mine a lasting steel monument to the fear that had guided it, like a prayer, to precisely where it had struck.

"*Aval lamah cazeh Ashkenazi* (But why so Ashkenazi)?"

I was sure he had waited to ask the question until just before starting to piss, so that he could then piss onto the asked question. Shai had stopped at the side of the gravel road to relieve himself, on our way along the mile or so from the far range back to the yard, where they had sent the two of us to grab more crates of SS109 ammunition after we had run through our last sooner than expected. Shai was my *zug barzel* ("iron pair"), my assigned buddy in the field, which meant we were responsible for knowing one another's whereabouts, that we would share a pup tent, and that we pups would play fetch together, too.

Shai struck five out of six in the drill this morning, and seemed regretful he had not torn the head off the iron man at three hundred with his first shot from prone, instead having managed it only on a retry. But he was not hung up over it because this had not been our first of these, and unlike me, he had performed well in the others, too. When we shot from prone untimed and with rested lungs, I excelled and Shai's marks were only middling. But he seemed not to lose much prowess under stress, and had well before today noticed how I did.

Ashkenazi, of course, is what I was. A Jew of Eastern European descent. But in this context, *Ashkenazi* is a poke, a pejorative employed by Mizrachim to mean an effete and bookish Jew, one devoid of backbone, of overdeveloped cranium and underdeveloped gonads. Shai was having a good time of it, because after all, he was our squad's other sharpshooter, and I imagined had some interest in thinking himself its best. And I felt in no position to challenge it, as he finished his piss stream without my answering, then turned to me still smirking as we kept on up the gravel. I touched my black left eye, where the rifle had stamped a scarlet mark of my infirmities this morning, and I thought about being Ashkenazi. Perhaps this stereotype was based on reality, and perhaps he was right about me in both senses of the word. I took notes in ballistics class, was obsessive about my form, exhaled twice before pulling, did not ever shoot without meaning it. Yet it seemed there was another ingredient Shai had in full supply, one I could not study up on, one that might explain why I shot my bullets with murderous precision when unhurried, but otherwise dumped them as bricks onto the sand.

And I thought about *lachatz nafshi*, another elegant term which translates as "spirit pressure" but has no real English match. *Lachatz nafshi* is "stress" written in bloody scarlet, the stress of being under fire, like I imagined our friend de Sales revealed himself not to have seen much of when he preached not ever to lose one's inner peace no matter how upset the whole world. *Lachatz nafshi* is when nothing looks the same as it did, and I thought I had come upon a trace of it when we crawled in gas masks and shot at iron men through clouded eyes. I had not yet seen truer *lachatz nafshi* than this, but had begun permitting myself to imagine where more waited.

But we had come to the yard now, not saying more along the way. It had not been an uncomfortable silence—Shai and I were weeks and months past those. We were each glad the other was there, and each knew the other was glad the other was there, and two know that when that is what silence means, neither breaks it unless he must, and now anyway here we were at the ammunition shelves. So we grabbed a couple crates each by their metal handles, and turned back around for the range, where the rest would be under the sun waiting for us to resupply them with the sacraments of life.

Getting back to the range with four fresh crates and the sun at our backs, we found that the others while waiting had switched to *yeveshim*—meaning "dry," and referring to any drill not involving wet combustion of live rounds through our barrels. Instead we made toys of our weapons and turned them on one another, to signify our fake hostility threaded orange plastic safety rods through them and out the end of the barrel, the rifle spitting out a rod of fire to show that these toys held nothing else, nothing wetter than plastic flames. Shai and I knew from a distance what the rest were up to when we saw them standing in a circle, rifles at their backs spitting orange flames to the sand. Within the circle would be another cockfighting ring, two men at two paces and then upon one another, each with one eye forced open and the other shut, the open eye shooting knives through his scope and the shut eye trimming away the world outside, as one must. The men tossing themselves about on command and their ears itching for the next call, while the others hooted and bet on their fortunes, only now and then choking on the rising dust.

"*Gilgul! Gilgul! Gilgul!*" As Shai and I approached, the commander called three rolls in a row, each man thrice tossing the world upside down over the sand, 1080 degrees of vertigo, landing on your stomach and searching down your scope with the open eye, restoring view of the enemy at two meters. As we made it to the circle, we found Shmuel winning the duel, vanquishing Valera, a Russian immigrant and the other sharpshooter of Shmuel's 2-*gimel*. Shmuel had spun himself over the earth and fixed a *maatzor rishon* (a quickie) before Valera finished his third roll, and so Shmuel had made it to one full movement ahead of him, now calling "*Aish!*" and his flame bearing fatally from prone.

I might have placed a bet on Shmuel had I arrived in time, but even without a stake, I felt a certain pride to see him win this cold war, as a Yankee does. And Valera was not my favorite: he shot angrily, and there was scarcely a mother on the yard whose reputation he had not impugned. But he had a presence with the men because he was brash, a strong shooter, and no *Ashkenazi*. Valera cursed now and threw a stone to the sky, calling for a rematch, though he would not get one as the next two names were called from the circle. Shmuel came to his feet and took his place in the ring without a word, nodding to the couple of men who clapped him on his shoulder as he rejoined. I knew Shmuel did not love Valera either, and I remembered Valera had edged him in an earlier duel—but Shmuel would not crow a word about evening the score, a higher road than I'd have taken.

There was another fight now anyway, Yossi and Tomer of 3-*gimel* taking their places in the ring before the dust had settled. I was offered a bet by Shai, and I favored Tomer—but I recalled I had just ten shekels left in my wallet back in the tent and was saving them for the *shekem*, the canteen we were allowed to visit on occasion for air-conditioning and ice cream bars. Ten shekels was good for at least one bar, and it was all I had, so I turned down Shai's wager even though it built his case I was an *Ashkenazi*. And we watched without horses in the race as the two men dropped and began to thrash about, the dust rising thick again as we clapped and hooted, the riddled iron men behind our backs at three hundred finding prayer for new life, praying this moment of peace might last.

26.

A moment of peace at the pool. It was summer at the pool, and I was wondering what you do if you are in the pool when *Tzeva Adom* comes. In the middle of the pool. If you are a little kid wearing neon arm floaties alone in the middle of the pool, still learning to swim, and on comes her first call of the four. And Izzy hacked into a massive watermelon and broke off huge slices, passed them around the table to us dripping, as we sheltered under the umbrella, the sun blazing on a gorgeous June day.

Izzy also passed around Bulgarian cheese, which he had put on the family account at Be'eri's *kol-bo* ("everything in it"), its general store, which had everything in it. I had not eaten this distinctive creamy briny cheese before Be'eri, but it was a favorite here. And because this taste had belonged to nothing, it did not need to leave anything behind to now be fallen in love with anew; and because this taste reminded me of nothing, it met no resistance in now reminding me of home.

And I chomped into the sweet watermelon and salty cheese and the taste of the hot sunscreen residue melting onto them from my fingers. Across the pool, kids took turns chucking themselves off the diving board into the clear deep end, acting out movie characters in midair. There went Arad off the board, because Arad could swim without arm floaties, and he acted out Channing Tatum from *Step Up*, which we had watched together after Shabbat dinner with Hebrew subtitles a few weeks back. Today was Shabbat again and I hoped to go run in the field alone later once the sun was low—but for the afternoon we were here, two thirds a watermelon still dripping under the umbrella, its seeds left swimming in a pool of red juice on the tray.

And last night I had been jolted awake to a *Tzeva Adom*, but it turned out to have been just in my dream, because she called once and twice, and I was not running fast enough, and when I ran faster, there was no third call and it was a cool and beautiful night and I was in my bed at the window overlooking the neighbor's green field and clay pots and the brown chickens he kept in the yard, asleep in the coop. And his rooster always crowed a couple hours early so it had to be the middle of the night still. And I was exhausted from the week because we had just finished our first stretch of days in Hebron, so I fell back asleep fast enough, but first I became aware I had now had one real *Tzeva Adom* and one imagined one, and then I became aware I was keeping count of these without trying to.

We had made it through most of the watermelon and Dotan jumped up from her seat to go swim and got her flippers and goggles on, even though she needed neither to swim because she had been raised in this pool. She tugged my wrist to come join her and we hopped in, but into the shallow end because she needed me to be standing firm for my role in our game.

"Throw me!" And as she loved, I hoisted her out of the water and held her high as she straightened herself, my shooting hand under her two knees brought together, my second hand under her collarbone, her two arms straight out to the sides ready to fly. And I launched her like a rocket toward the deep end, where the other kids played, but not far enough to hit any of them, and she sailed and flapped her wings, and laughed, all the way to the surface. And her long hair floated back to the surface, and she shook it off and swam back to me and called for another. Now and then Arad asked for these, too, and he loved them also, but he was heavier, did not ever get quite as far or as high in the air, and did not ever try to fly away from the surface.

Arad and I did a few, but before long he went back to his friends and it was me and Dotan again. We stayed awhile after Izzy and Noga had walked home from under the umbrella, the other kids still jumping off the board and acting out movies till the surface stopped them, Dotan flying and laughing till the same. My shoulders ached, but I kept going, because I loved these as much as Dotan did, and because I knew when my shoulders were sore tomorrow as I unlocked my rifle and got on the bus back to Hebron, they would remind me of where I had been.

The *adhan*, the Muslim call to prayer, flooded the city streets and it overtook my senses, because it would be a crude untruth to say this call was merely and only heard. The call came from outside then inside me and it buckled my knees where it rose through them, owing to the way it came from all sides here in the heart of the city, and owing even more to what he called, what he sang. I knew not a word of his call, and wanted never for his prayer's meaning to shrink the way the Hebrew prayers of my childhood had shrunk years later once I came to know the words within them. Because when he sang the *adhan*, these new linguistic parts of my brain stayed dark and these old primal ones—these truest ones—took it all. These had no interest in the inexact science of interpreting his call; only in the far more exact science of letting it mean the grief and trembling and yearning in his voice, letting it mean the way he embedded the whole of himself within it and propelled it from the tower, letting it mean the way his voice came to me once and again from the next tower and again from the far one, the all of them echoing from the walls of my room and filling it to bursting, the all of these three voices like a harmony of three Christian, Jewish, and Muslim brothers knowing together to sing the very same beautiful song.

Never had I heard these three voices sing, never in this way. My first *adhan* of memory came in 2006, a guided college tour of Israel. Day one off the plane, straight to Jerusalem under our jet lag, then to the Old City's rooftops to take in the panorama of the hills before sunset. And from our rooftop we saw the Temple Mount in the orange light, and our rabbi spoke of what came before us, and then as the sun set in the west, in rolled the *adhan* from the east, distant but strong. And we all heard it, and the rabbi raised his voice as one raises a gragger on Purim, and spoke with vigor, to drown out the call of his enemy. And he kept on till the call faded, after which he returned to calm, because he knew how long it would go, had heard it many times before.

And so now was my first time hearing the *adhan* in this way, some far echo of a Jewish voice within, alongside a Muslim one. But even so, this *adhan* was like the delicious Bulgarian cheese of Be'eri; since it reminded me of nothing, it met no resistance in now reminding me that I was hemmed in all the way, that I was not safe, and that I was somewhere I did not want to be. And it was not fair for this gorgeous prayer to mean the way that my palms perspired and locked tighter on my weapon, that my neck swiveled around this empty room and feared the walls around me, that I felt his call as an assault and longed for it to stop gripping the city's air. But my preconscious adrenaline centers now firing their cylinders were unconcerned with the luxury of fair; they were truer than that. In here I was without schooling, without letters to my name, alone with what they left behind.

In here I knew no more than a few words—or rather one sentence, because I did not know which words meant what within it. Words I could not rearrange to design any other message, one rigid chain of them, the one each of us was taught and was not expected to have to say, but to have ready in case: *Wakef walla-anna batuchak*. In Arabic: Stop or I will shoot. And there was a reason for this, because we were soldiers and not diplomats, and these words might save my life or that of a friend. But I wondered if they could not have taught us each word instead of just the chain, so that within my mind I could rearrange these word magnets into more poems than just this one. Because the people of this city had heard this poem before from people like me, and not heard others. And when they saw me, I imagined they assumed I carried this poem, and no others, and this assumption would have been correct. And they said nothing to me when I walked past in the streets, clad in ballistic vest and they in T-shirts. And though they looked at me proudly, I came to avoid looking back, because I imagined they knew I had only one thing to say to them.

27.

"**H**adaf!"
  "*Hadaf!*"

The others seemed upset about this and there was a fight brewing, but I could not look away. I was alone now, more at ease than in my first shift in Hebron perched two floors above an intersection watching the street below, a checkpoint to search passing vehicles for weapons or explosives, my men flagging down cars one by one, I the sharpshooter watching over, crosshairs ready on the other men below.

This shift was away from there, in a solo tower at an outlying base, far enough to hear the *adhan* only as a distant prayer in late afternoon. At fifty meters was a village in the valley below, and at its edge a pack of boys, about Arad's age, playing soccer on a concrete field. When I started the shift, I had raised my scope to scan all around and there was just the village below and the gray lot, which stayed empty a couple hours till the boys showed up with the black-and-white ball.

And I smiled because now I had a game to watch, and a view from above. I was near enough to watch without my scope, far enough they could see me but pretend I was not there. When I was a kid, we did the same thing to the playground supervisors, pretended they were not watching so we could play the way we wanted. And I was happy now that they ignored me altogether as they split into teams, and swarmed the ball and shoved at one another while the goalies clapped and shouted from behind. The goals they stood in were just the spaces between two metal poles, not like our goals which had big white nets that made it easy to see a score. And now the ball had been kicked past the goalie and they were fighting over whether it had gone in, which was another thing I would not have had to fight over as a child.

They were shouting and the word they had in common sounded like *hadaf*, which had to mean "goal." It was a new word, the fifth I knew and the first I had learned from a native, and I was happy they taught it to me but happier still that they continued to pretend I was not there. Before long they had come to some decision and the ball was live again, and a boy freed it from the crowd and they tugged his shirt from behind but could not stop him from breaking out ahead and sinking a beautiful goal, and "*Hadaf!*"

It was *hadaf* for certain, because this was the same word he shouted as he raised his arms and ran back to his boys, who shouted it, too. And the ball was rolling again, and the same boy attacked it and broke loose, and he had a fan now in the tower. He scored again, and it seemed his team was running away with it, but before long the sun was setting on the hills so they took the ball and started heading home. You could tell the winning team by the way they jumped together when they ran off the field, like we had done, too. And I wished they would keep playing, because I had another couple hours to go. But it was getting to be too dark to see without infrared, so I remembered to switch to my Lior, then looked through it for another scan of my environment, to see if any of it had changed while I was away at the game.

As before, they were returning to the game. They were only boys playing hopscotch, numbered squares, stones in hand. A group of children fallen still on our patrol's approach, holding tongues and stones. They would not throw the stones as on yesterday's patrol. These were legal stones, as a metal bat in the trunk when accompanied by ball and glove. There was no cause to grip my weapon tighter, none to stop, none to watch them any longer than to see they held the stones to signal they were only playing hopscotch, only little boys, returning to the game. The stones would not be hurled at our backs, clunk and patter on our armor, like first rain; we would not turn to find them, four in all, shooting anger, the youngest handing weapons to his brother who was grown enough to sling them, a second volley at our eyes and gone around the corner, leaving only leaden echoes from the vacant houses, clunk, patter. There was no reason for unease, as they were only boys. All four were grown enough to sling the stones, but held them for us as we passed and then a safe distance after, without a word over the echoes of the day before.

28.

Inside the pillbox were four unworn prayer books, like the Holy Bible one finds waiting in the nightstand in a roadside motel. Like the men before us, we left them untouched, because a man not inclined to prayer under normal conditions was even surer to avoid it here, where his new impulse to piety would be most disquieting to us others. So by tacit accord we let them sit, in the circle in which they had been arranged like a shrine, and we placed no wear on their pages, leaving them unspoiled for the next men to come.

Nor did we say much, because there was a high sense of exposure despite the reinforced concrete walls of the cylindrical tower in which we hid. The armored carrier had driven just fifteen minutes from base into Hebron, but when the four of us jumped from its doors and hurried inside the tower walls, there was the sensation of inhaling and submerging in a closed cylinder, swinging metal door latched and sealed, watertight.

Forty-eight hours sealed inside and never more exposed to outside, in the way that a submarine crew descending to the black is conscious always of crush depth, the depth at which the vessel can no longer resist the crippling force of the water and is crumpled like a tin can.

I never understood, as a child, how people slept on submarines. I would always be thinking of crush depth.

And so to sleep inside the pillbox, at this depth in the city, was the hard part. On the bottom floor beneath the spiral staircase were two bunks, one above the other as shelves on the wall. No space between each bunk and the staircase to sit up straight, nor to lie flat due to the tight curve of the wall. Instead one curled with his back to the wall, and hoped not to wake to an alarm, and sit up. In principle one could sleep when not in the pair guarding above, but that asked much, when one could spend the time at rest instead.

It was easier above, where there was more space after the stairway ended, and fresh air coming through the slits in the eight armored windows. Unless we were sleeping, which was the hard part, we sat above even when it was not our turn, and played chess without time and without comment, either one of which would distract from our purpose in the game with the brittle plastic pieces that were far more tired than the books below.

29.

By all accounts, the streets of Hebron were found wanting in their accommodation of our armored personnel carriers. Unlike the grid of interstates we had inaugurated to surround the city, its inner streets were unyielding to modernity. They were narrow, irregular and winding, and their sad old limestone could be heard to crunch and shudder, occasionally gasp, as our steel treads rolled over them. Mercifully, by gift of modern engineering, our carrier's shocks ensured an easy ride unmoved by these agitations, while our treads kept up the work to flatten them, to smooth them at the edges.

There was little talk inside the carrier while it was working. There were the crunching, sighing, rasping, gasping city streets beneath us. Rare for anyone to wish to speak above it all, rarer anyone who wished to hear him. But there was, I found, still some pattern to it: the quiet was thicker on the ride to an assignment in the city, than on the one returning from it.

Between the ride headed there and the ride headed back, the first was the longer, and the more humid. The ride headed there was not like the inmate's ride in the police car back from his proceedings, when he was free at least to be relieved of his synthetic suit jacket, loosen his oppressive necktie. No, this was the car to take him there, where his formal dress would play a vital role in his defense before the jurors who, unfailingly in plain clothes, were waiting.

And so in this carrier, the one headed there, if he thought about it, it would bring him not to loosen his suit but to secure it nearer. And so he drew his armor tighter, even if that brought its plates against his rib cage and limited his lungs' expansion, and he saw no paradox in that retreat or in its comfort. Even if he never gave it a thought, it was not hard for him or anyone to see that our green *kerami* armor offered refuge, one more sanctuary for our hiding, always hiding.

We wore our rigid suits so they could not kill us, of course, though in Hebron all parties knew that threat was relatively mild, not like the far more pressing urgency to make it so they could not see us. Not in our eyes or hearts or other parts we treasured, the ones that needed hiding.

Our suits ensured that when they saw us, they would pierce no farther than the same green suit unique to none of us, would not penetrate or rend the vital parts of each of us they covered, would not roll, pitch, or yaw through his defenseless parts that loved to dance or study poetry, nor his that played guitar and sang, or played soccer with his little brother, nor his part that kissed his *bubbe* on the cheek, or pushed Dotan high laughing on the swing, nor the one that got home safe and was embraced by his mother. And not the part of me that held the memory that I had come because of Avi. These parts required adamant, bulletproof protection and would get it. And so in this carrier he tightened more the strap on his *kerami* vest, which bore no name badge, now breathing easier.

This quiet unmarking of the individual was marked, and in this way we were, it seemed, acutely timid—childlike, even. On the one hand, this was our first deployment. Maybe this was simply what it meant for young soldiers to band together against what meets them. On the other, I could not get that thought to feel quite honest. For instance, though I had not been in a war of defense, I imagined there to be this difference: in such a war, if I held my rifle and prepared to use it, it still would be horrific, yet it could surely be with my whole heart, holding in it those I loved. But here, when I prepared to act, I could not except in such a way as to forget them. To hide these things to me most special, to hide the parts of me that held them.

And so we hid them, which is to say we hid ourselves. Behind our sprawling base's walls that loomed over darkened streets surrounding, within the concrete pillboxes that claimed the high points of the hills to hold dominion over rows of houses, inside the sluggish armored carriers on patrol among the dusty cars they could have rolled right over, and most preserving, in our green *kerami* life vests encircled by onlooking T-shirts.

Yet to hide is an exhausting thing. An unsustainable one.

Which was the essence: this green armor could not be pierced except by those who also wore it. Its preservation required only our agreement, or rather, less: only quiet. It asked so little of each one of us that not to give it was beyond an insult—a transgression. With all one's training, and all one's men depending on him for it, it would be a failing rare indeed for one not to find it in himself to give this fraction.

30.

A new checkpoint, not in the streets among the people where they looked at me, but a couple floors above where they did not. It was easier up here without their eyes on me, but still I resented my commanders for doing this to me, because first they had trained me to fire with clinical precision, and now planted me here with instructions to be the first to act if anything should go wrong down below. These were simple instructions, but my own mind crisscrossed over them while I lay above. How it would look in the moment before a passing man became a deadly threat; how I would know to fire not too soon but not too late; the assumption that if my eye left the scope any moment, it would be the wrong one.

So I left behind all worlds other than the one in my scope: at its red center the man driving to the checkpoint, around him my men flagging down the vehicle to search it, the man's two hands staying on the steering wheel, where my men and I could see them.

And a rickety white van had stopped at the checkpoint, the driver's face appearing at red center as he lowered the tinted window. Two men stayed with him and two went toward the trunk, and his hands stayed where I could see them, until the two men had shut the trunk's two white doors and the other two waved him on. His face and hands now disappeared behind the window glass, and his feet, from somewhere I could not see them, took the van onward.

As the next vehicle approached, I wished to be below with the others, because I knew something would go wrong. And when it did, down there my trauma would be shared, softened in its collectivity, not solitary and soaked through with having acted too late. But in truth, I had it easier than the men below, because they had many decisions to make, and up here I had one: fire or not. Shoot the man if and only if he became a deadly threat—but act not too soon and not too late. So far I had seen only "too soon," but this man sat one meter from my friends at the window, his hands for now where I could see them. If "too soon" became "now," then "too late" would come not one breath later, let alone the two I always needed.

He was not far, much closer than the iron men at three hundred, and this shot was easy but the timing was not. We were given no training in watching real men to determine when they became enemies, when "too soon" matured to "now"— but it was clear this was the most important thing left for me to learn. So I began on my own, studying the innocent men so when a guilty one came, I would see the difference. And the next window lowered and at red center was the man, and there was a thrill in watching him, discovering him.

There was much to observe from here, where he did not know I was. I studied each man's magnified form, and began with his hands, because he would not get from "now" to "too late" without them. But then recalled I was most concerned with knowing when "too soon" moved to "now"—and this would come first in his face, not hands, so I began to study all it did, taking most interest in his eyes, where I imagined he would show himself. I began looking there always, studying innocent eyes so I would know guilty ones. I searched them for violence, ready to act when I found it. For now I saw none. Anxious eyes in this car and resentful eyes in the next, and more in the ones to come. But no violent eyes. Not yet.

Cars passed and the day ended and a new checkpoint began, and I came to feel I had seen enough innocent eyes to understand what guilty ones would not look like, but they kept showing me more. Still I could not take my crosshairs off the next man because any moment I did would be the wrong one. And though I did not feel it at first, it grew difficult putting at red center another man's innocent eyes, in the same way it was difficult looking back at the men in T-shirts on the street—even though this man did not see me. But it became worse on occasion, when something in his face made me feel he knew I was there. This was worse than being on the street below, because to hold a crosshairs on a man who sees you is harder than just to look at him. But then if he saw me, it was more likely he was guilty, because a guilty man had to be more likely than an innocent to know, or to believe, that someone was above. And now came a surge of suspicion that he had to be guilty because he saw me.

But I also could not stand his eyes on me while I aimed at him, because it made me feel exposed, and guilty. And I wanted him to be guilty, because if he were guilty, then I would not be. And then came the first time I noticed my trigger finger itching for release.

It quivered when my men shouted at the driver, or tossed things in the car during the search. And when the air grew tense below, I was glad to have studied all the innocent eyes before, and watched his for violence. But found none: anxious eyes would come to fearful and resentful ones to angry, but never to violent, from "too soon" to "now." And at shift's end it was even harder to come down to the street where they saw me again, because I was sure they knew where I had been, and their glares produced a drowning shame in me, a vertigo that made me envy their T-shirts and hate my vest—and hate them, too, for being innocent when I was not.

Then above again I began not only to look for "now" but to await it, surer than ever it was on its way. And after all this time being "too soon" and all the men in T-shirts who knew I was guilty, the time was arriving for one of them to be, so I could show I was not.

Then came the first time I was sure a man was about to turn guilty, and I took a first breath, for my enemy, to anticipate the "now," because once "now" came, there would be no time for two. But I stopped myself before the second breath, the one for me.

Then came the first time my mind saw the trigger moving, the easiest shot of my career, painting the windshield red. And the story was so red, it broke the rule that a story must have a beginning, middle, and end, because I did not see what provoked the shot or what followed. Only the middle part, the release. When it filled the sight, red windshield, bare of provocation and consequence, I pulled my eye away—but the man was still there, one meter from my friends, so I returned to it, because I was lucky this moment had not already been the wrong one. And the man kept his hands where I could see them, and his face disappeared behind the glass and he got on his way.

Then at red center was the next man and his windshield, and he dropped his hands from the wheel to somewhere I could not see them, but he was just opening the door, and stepped out toward the trunk of his van and both hands again where I could see them. Two men searched the trunk and from up here I could not see inside, just them behind, and he was guarding something.

One man stopped him while the other searched, and I could not see inside but now a thing fell out to the earth, at the edge of my world which held him at center. Another thing fell, and they were planks of wood, and his eyes grew angry, and another fall, and my men shouting and fists raised and a wooden clock, coming to rest with the planks, at the edge of the world. Then screaming inches from one another and I saw the trigger move again but no red windshield, just him, lying in the dirt behind the van, alone between my men in his white T-shirt. And I stopped my breath, because all of him was where I could see him. And his clock hid nothing either, lying faceup on the earth.

He was a woodworker, I thought, after we had finished and let him go. His clock, and his wares, so he guarded them. It meant I was guilty, and wished for the next man to be guilty, so I could be not. And the next man's face and windshield appeared at red center, and my men headed for the trunk and I wondered if a plight like mine afflicted them below. They were just nineteen, so being guilty may have been as foreign to them as to me, searching for violence, finding it in the corners of your eyes, wanting it gone from you, wanting the next man guilty so you could be not. And when they shouted at the other men or struck them or things fell to the earth, this could have been why, because they were ways to call the other man guilty to make yourself not, and if I were down there, I would have valued the option. And though at first I had it easier up here than them, I now saw otherwise, because they had these milder ways to make the other man guilty, and I only one.

Then their voices were raised again below and silently I added mine. Daring him to light up a flash of violence in his eye, to bring us to "now"—but in spite of us he did not either, would not bring us anywhere but "too soon." And I held him firm where he belonged at red center, waiting, pleading, even as I saw at the edge of the world the face of the clock, and the time it told.

Home, and free of my rifle in the open field. *We were only boys*, came the thought as a glimmer through a thick night sky. Not grown men. Only boys had the need to stay guiltless. Only boys had the need to make the other man guilty, so they could be not.

31.

If we had a grown man among us, it was Shmuel, and if he had a grave defect, it was exactly that. It was that he thought too much, too hard, and exposed himself to the consequences, which meant exposing us to them, too. Not one of us had failed to uphold the mission, but if one was closest, it was Shmuel, by now known as our resident *yafeh nefesh*. This meant "beautiful soul," a slur whose twin fricatives fell with special friction from the lips, attaching to a soldier whose hands could not be dirtied, whose sticky conscience made him weak at times the mission could ill afford it.

Now he had started up again as we rode in the carrier—and not even on the ride back, as would have been fairer, but the ride there.

"The Talmud teaches that sleep is a fraction of death."

Beside me on the metal seat in the back of the carrier—the one headed there. Facing straight, the direction we were headed, and in quiet English, so that I alone was charged with its recognition.

In his defense, lungs pressed against his vest to draw the heavy stale air of the car headed there, one returns to the ground floor of his hierarchy of needs, which for Shmuel included oxygen and moral reconciliation, neither well on hand to him in the back of the carrier. But not now, Shmuel, don't tell horrid stories while we're about to begin eating. Yet he could not turn it off.

"The idea is that death is sleep's most extreme manifestation," he expounded, following a humid pause, inferring need of further substance. "That unconsciousness is a form of death, different only in degree."

The carrier was lurching on the cobblestone and my green helmet riding back and forth again, though I was certain I had just secured it—so I saw to it as was needed. But he had not finished.

"And the Talmud's lessons can be acted on, always," he continued, in quiet, facing straight. "So in my mind it's not a warning about unconsciousness in sleep, but in waking."

He waited again for me, but still he had asked no question, so I looked out into the wall where in the rear of a police car there might have been windows. Wiped the grease again from my temples. Metal grates on the ceiling.

"The fraction is said to be one sixtieth. One sixtieth of death."

His voice lower, as if resigned to not being answered, but steady, even as we hit a rough incline and the floor rocked while we began to climb it. And still not a question: he had moved to a pronouncement, leaving space for no rejoinder, no saving answer.

Then in the silence something burst. As though the airtight walls of our submersible had at last sprung leaks and my life vest of no use against the water rushing in around us, alert faintly to the sounds of life from outside but powerless to reach it, trapped by the metal walls around me and the iron grating on the ceiling, and in my state I had not even noticed that the carrier had stopped and waited, before the doors were thrown wide open, and a rush of air, clear light streaming in from a high hot sun above us—we had reached the hilltop, where the tower waited.

Time to move, came the calls from the men in green outside the carrier. Time to move.

And my eyes found not this hilltop and the tower, but the

next over, there, a smaller hill, a naked one, a couple of boys were running on it, breathing deep. I could not see for certain in the distance, but it seemed one wielded a wand and he was breathing deep, blowing rainbow bubbles from the liquid, and they were running in the sun beneath them.

The men in green were waiting to begin their other ride, the one headed home, calling, and it was time to move.

Outside, above the next hill, was a bright blue summer day and from here the bubbles were invisible, if they existed, yet as I jumped to the pavement and before I turned, there came an instant I was sure that in the sharp clear daylight, even in the distance, the rays lit up for me the image of the iridescent bubbles that shimmered high and drifted, up to the sun.

32.

It should not have surprised me when I descended from the lookout and was face-to-face with a man I had just held at red center. He might have lived two blocks away—but he looked different now, younger to my naked eye, because my scope had hardened his face, made him look old. He wore a T-shirt like the others, and looked at me proudly like them, too. I could not return his gaze and it was unsafe to stand here without rejoining my men, but for a moment I stayed. I did not know if he had seen me above or knew what I had done to him. I wanted to explain I was sorry, but I had not learned this word and I imagined he knew that also. So for this once I let him look at me, and looked back far longer than was safe, like staring into the sun. I took in every part of his face, and told myself I would remember it. And told him, in my heart, in a way I believe he understood, that I would tell the story of the day I met him.

33.

His call came so whole that in my heart I was sure I understood. Clearer here at the edge of the city than in the heart of the streets below. Not the flooding, disorienting, drowning call from all directions, but a long, mournful, unbroken call from one. One voice from the city.

The *adhan* swept over us again and it brought a restfulness over the houses below, but the restfulness was not ours. Today was Friday, soon to be Shabbat, the day of rest, but we stood a line of soldiers spaced apart along Worshipper's Way, the path that led from Kiryat Arba down to the Cave of the Patriarchs below.

It had been a Friday like today, November 15, 2002, when soldiers of the Nachal Brigade, ours, came under ambush here on the path. A company of settlers made their way up the path from the cave after Friday evening prayers welcoming the Sabbath, and then the all-clear bell rang at the settlement gates, to signal all had made it safely home. The soldiers who had protected their way were still out in the open, starting home, when a trio of hidden gunmen burst into fire from behind their backs. Waited for the loud sounding of the all-clear bell, before the quiet clicking of rifles out of safe mode.

Patish cham, "hot hammer," rang out from every radio in the region, the code that fire has erupted on our forces. Colonel Dror Weinberg, ranking commander of the Hebron Brigade, was raced to the scene in his armored jeep and shot dead as he emerged. In the hours that followed, the ambushers killed twelve before being cornered and gunned down—just three militants, moving among the roofs and windows of the city they knew so well. The three had been friends in their early twenties at Hebron's polytechnic university, studying engineering. They had designed careful schemes for the attack, studied the battleground before it became one, planned it as a martyrdom operation, written their traditional wills. The ambush site, just across the way, became known after in both Hebrew and Arabic as the Alley of Death, a fixed neighbor on the far side of the brightly lit Worshipper's Way, where it cast its shadow.

Today it was late afternoon and the shadows of the worshippers on the path were getting longer, but it would be some time before we reached the all-clear bell. They were making their way down to the cave to begin, out of Kiryat Arba's narrow gate and down the narrow path, into the city that surrounded. *All the world is a very narrow bridge.* And yet as we watched the worshippers wind their way down the path, arm in arm, there was a restfulness that crept in with the *adhan*, because there were glimmers of our work being done. It was the final stretch of our provisional deployment here, to this city incompatible with peace within ourselves, and we were looking forward to leaving it behind us, till the next time we were drawn back again.

We were spaced far enough apart that each soldier was in conversation only with himself, but near enough that none of us was alone. There on the path walked a father and his young son, a black rifle on the father's back, the two holding hands so their shadow shared the rifle, like Dotan and me on the day we met. I thought of my father, who was thinking of me, and next time we spoke on the phone, I needed to tell him of this father and son. I needed to tell him they returned me to the Saturdays he had walked me as a boy to our synagogue, hand in hand across the bridge and through the park, carrying nothing, until we were almost back home and he held me up to pick lemons from the high branches of the neighbor's tree, to squeeze for juice in the afternoon.

I had drifted into an unsafe peacefulness, watching father and son and their long shadow, when a grown figure came behind the boy, in his wake. Headed away from me toward the cave, a white kipah and blond head on two rigid shoulders.

It was Shimon.

He had told us at Michve Alon, of course, that he was born and raised in a settlement on a hill above the city of Hebron. He was home now, had finished his service and returned to his family and places of prayer. There on the path was Shimon's unarmed back, and protecting it was my rifle, the one his law had given me.

"Shimon!"

He was thirty meters down the path but spun around like I had never left his sight, white tzitzit in the sun as he turned. "Binyamin! *Shabbat shalom.*"

It was him—I had known from behind but wished to see his face, hear his voice, to know it again. I did not know what to say, and then he saw my rifle and called, "You have become a sharpshooter!"

And though I had not said another word, I felt a hot liquid pride well up within. But with this same welling I wanted to scream at him. I wanted him to know I had this rifle because of him and his law. I wanted him to know about the windshield and the clock, to know about the man I met when I came down. I wanted him to know about Dror and Noam and all the things his rifle had taken from me that could not return, and that it had not just taken them but replaced them with itself, come to occupy the same places in my heart, my hands, and that in these places the rifle was all I had left. I wanted him to know there was no difference between my pride in my rifle and my grief in what it had taken, because these were the same thing. I wanted him to know. But I did not know how to tell him, and I found no words to give him but those I now called. *Shabbat shalom.*

"*Kol hakavod,*" he pronounced to me. "*Haroveh yoshev yafeh alecha, ach sheli* (The rifle sits beautifully upon you, brother)."

And my liquid pride spilled out over the sides of me, and my grief spilled, too, because these were the same thing. And my head stood high in the air, because his words made me surge with pride, and I loved him. I had so much to tell him and wished to begin—but he had turned his back to me and was already gone, trusting his back to my protection as I stood alone and he disappeared, down the path and toward the cave to join his congregation.

34.

The day that Shimon left me full of pride, it was not as if I wished, or even could envision, that we would ever bring an end to our occupation. Not while it and I were codependent. Not in the checkpoints, the fruitless searches for weapons and vindication, the guiltlessness of ours which we carried in and brutally imposed upon them in order to be able to stay blameless. And not the day I saw the rainbow bubbles drift up high above to where we could not contain them. Not until well after I was far from the occupation's protection, its light tricks and distortions, and the green suit's comforting constriction.

Breathing deep. I remember the two boys running on the crested hill, breathing deep. *Shalem, shalom.* Wholeness, peace. Two names, one *shoresh.* I hold them both together as I remember Shmuel without an answer in the back of the carrier, the fraction that it cost us, the fraction that we gave it.

Part III

35.

Freedom is nothing but the distance between the
hunter and the hunted.
—Bei Dao, "Accomplices"

To be a soldier, so far as I had pieced together, was to be in a perpetual place of yearning. Not one of fatigue, or filth, or fear. These came and they stayed, had the key to my house so they rarely made a show of knocking first. But when they departed again, as they would, I was reminded that they were but overstaying neighbors in my own house, which was named yearning.

And so I smiled when I learned our first full deployment would be to the Gazan border region of Kisufim, because *kisufim* is a literary word meaning "yearnings." I knew that Kisufim's crossing into Gaza had been the main route into the Gush Katif settlement bloc before Israel's withdrawal in 2005; that Kisufim remained among the most volatile stretches of the border, beset by Hamas rocket assaults and attempts to breach the wall or cross through tunnels running underneath. I knew also that Kisufim was only several kilometers from Be'eri, so when we got the news late in our days in Hebron, I called Izzy the same night. A rarity, because normally I would not invite the sound of his voice until I was almost home, and he was picking me up from the bus station to bring me through the yellow gate.

Mazal tov, came Izzy's voice on the phone. That's right next door.

Yes, it is so close. Too bad they won't let me come home for lunch. How far is Kisufim from Be'eri?

Depends where you are within it, but only about eight kilometers.

The longest eight kilometers, I said to myself, while saying to him, it will be wonderful to be deployed so close to home.

He agreed, and told me how proud he would be to let the others know his son was serving nearby on the border.

And we hung up, but only after he said he would tell Noga, and the children, and Noga's mother and father, who also lived in Be'eri in their own house down the way. And only after he said he was glad I had called to tell him, because now he would have time to pick up meat at the market so when I made it home for Shabbat, they could have an *al-ha-aish* for me, to honor my next chapter.

To deploy to Kisufim, I already imagined, would be different. There, if I prepared to use my rifle, it could be with my whole heart. Despite the horrors of it—or I should say, precisely because of them—I could keep my loved ones in my heart, there with me, as I did it. And what a difference.

That Friday evening we lingered at the playground. On the way home from the station, Izzy had told me all was set for the *al-ha-aish* tomorrow, the fridge stocked with meat and hummus and my favorite red schug from Dorit, the mother in the house next door whose recipe was the best I ever tasted, who had made me a big jar as her blessing for Kisufim. And after we got home and I had cleaned up and locked away my rifle, together we sat with the other families in the *cheder ochel*, with challah from Be'eri's ovens and vegetables from its fields. And once Dotan was done eating, she jumped up and tugged at my wrist, like she would do when she was ready to play in the pool, because after Shabbat dinner we would go outside to the playground, too.

Arad joined and the three of us went to the patio to stop at the dessert tables, which were set up outside in summertime. They ate cookies off the table where we stood, and I did, too, before we moved on to the playground just beyond. Arad joined his friends on the jungle gym while Dotan ran to the swing and called for a push.

I stepped onto the sand and gave a big push, and she flew and laughed.

Most Friday evenings I would stay at the playground just a short time before going home to get off my feet, but tonight the air was warm and I decided I would stay as long as she liked. We stayed well past dark and I lost track of how long we had been there, and Dotan had not kept track either. After some time Arad and the boys left the jungle gym, and Izzy and Noga walked past on the path home and waved. For a while after, it was just Dotan and me under the lights that ran along the playground and the path, she facing away flying on the swing she loved, I standing behind.

36.

"Can you believe they're paying us to play laser tag?" Shmuel asked as they rigged a MILES combat simulation system all over his body. I studied while they layered him in black sensors on his chest, back, shoulders, head, because these black marks were the places I would be able to kill him when it was time.

"Can't believe they're not paying us more," I said before they rigged me up also, and now he studied while I took on rows of black lesions of my own. I looked down at them nakedly, chest and arms sprouting nodes of mortality, each one a new affliction.

"Let my people go, or it will get worse," Shai threatened from behind, grinning when I turned to face him.

"Wait, you believe in God, Shai?"

"One that does what we tell Him to."

It was another poem from the laureate, but he had not made much of it, already studying the lesions of the next man down. And we were out of time to peel back the layers anyway, because they had fitted our rifles with the laser emitters now, too, so instead of theologizing with Shai, I took a last study of his new mortal boils, before it was time to become mute and afraid of one another, and be scattered from our tower to the four corners of the earth.

At Tze'elim, Israel's premier school of urban warfare, out past the classrooms lies the jewel of Baladia, a city at the treacherous intersection of theory and practice. Risen from the sand with the generous assistance of the United States, Baladia is the Middle East's most tortured city, born an amalgam of the darkest corners of all the others. An irredeemable dystopia stretching five thousand acres in painstaking replication of an Arab town under eternal siege, Baladia is surely haunted, though to call it a ghost town would be unkind to ghost towns, which had once been alive before they were dead.

The first blasted house we rolled past at the city's edge had been spray-painted "Welcome to Chicago" in thick red Hebrew. It was Baladia's affectionate second name, but there was no sister city sign, because Baladia's city hall had no mayor, its soccer field had no children, and even its cemetery had no dead, because here no one ever died, all they did was fight.

It was our season now and I set off across the city with Valera, because they had not let us choose our friends in this dispersion, and we had drawn the short straws and would be the terrorists holding hostages at the city core. Baladia was our turf, so we were given a move-in period before the attack, to acquaint ourselves with the schoolyards and alleys, the places the enemy would need to discover on the fly under our fire. Valera and I and our men were on the move when a recorded *adhan* came on from the minarets, green crowns in the daylight. It filled the streets as we kept moving past the empty homes where we had been raised, and as it struck, we began shouting over it before remembering it was ours, too. Before long, our call still thick in the air around us, we had found the building we would occupy and began to set our nest, another layer to the simulation of attacking a city, and defending one.

They were coming now, and we had the hostages in two rooms on the second floor, and I stayed in one and watched the window with the others at my back. Then heard gunfire, and the blanks were not as loud as live rounds, and gave less recoil, but still their bursts filled the air. The enemies had not taken the street I watched over, and once I heard noise from the floor below, it was time to watch the doorway, too, and then came the buzzing between bursts, also from the floor below. It was the loud grating tone the MILES system emitted after a fatal strike to the wearer, whose weapon was deactivated now, and who could quiet the tone only by lying down until the end of the exercise.

Then they were in the hallway and I had no more use for the window. They would not throw a grenade because we had hostages in here, so I crouched in the far corner in full view of the room, sight trained at the edge of the doorway where they would appear. I knew their choreography for entering a room in pairs, the first man's barrel in and to the room's far side, second man over his outside shoulder in and near. Then a black barrel at the doorway, and he came and I fired and the second man a half step behind and fallen, too, and I kept shooting and the system was letting me so I must still be alive and now the hard metallic wails rising through the whole small room, two of them at the doorway, one of my own in the near corner, all three in harmony at the same tone.

They were on the floor, but one of them, the first to fall at the door, could not get his vest to stop. It was Shai, but I did not know him, and his vest was supposed to turn off once he was on his back but there was something wrong with it and it would not stop, and I watched him twist on his back and stomach trying to end it, before he gave up and lay still, the other two quiet now but Shai's final tone filling up the doorway, waiting for the others who were farther down the hall. Just a couple left in the room now, and more of them were coming from the hallway, and another black barrel at the edge of the door.

"What else you like here? These ones any good?"

"No, I'd say try those instead." I pointed him away from

the bitter Bissli snacks and toward the buttery Bamba, a better introduction to the land of milk and honey. Harris from Alabama was a private first class in the United States Marine Corps, and he had never seen the letters printed on these alien treats, apart from the loud red ones he passed this morning at the edge of Baladia, to him no friendlier than the Arabic tagged on the houses farther inside.

We were back from our skirmish and free for an hour at Tze'elim's canteen, where we had run into Marines who were about to go paint the town red again after their first exercise this morning. Since the Americans had helped create Baladia, they came by often to ravage it, too, like these boys who were on their way to Afghanistan to apply an eighth year of shock and awe, and had stopped here to study up beforehand. For us, Baladia was a city in the strip to the west, but for them, it might become Kandahar, because Baladia's thirst was always being quenched in new colors, reoutfitted by its pillagers in effigy of whichever real city they were sighting next.

We had gotten our snacks now and sat down at the canteen tables, and he introduced me to Flores from Los Angeles, not far from where I was raised.

"How you end up here anyway, brother?" asked Harris after Flores and I shook hands. "You American or Israeli?"

"I'm Jewish."

"Oh."

I had said it a bit defensively without meaning to, though I was glad that ended it, because if he had kept asking, I did not know what else I would say.

"You were right, these are great, like peanut butter Cheetos," Harris said after a quiet moment munching on his Bamba, and I nodded back, munching on mine, which I had decided to get, too, instead of Bissli, this time. Harris rubbed his fingers between grabs and dusted my rifle sitting on the bench, which was fine.

"Congrats on bin Laden," I commented after another bite, because the Americans had gotten him a couple months ago in May, and I had not seen one since.

"Double-tap, motherfucker." Flores came back, and held his hand up for a high five. I had not thought he would let me in like this, so I gave him a strong one, and as we clapped hands high in the air, I felt a warmth for these boys, too, and a wish we could sit for longer together, before we all had to go. And we went on talking about the war awhile, but before long they were due in Chicago. As they got going, it occurred to me it must have been one of them, an American, who first gave Baladia that name, the way old naval explorers would name strange new shores after home in case they would not see it again. I was not sure what to say, and the thing I found as they stood to go was "Thank you for your service."

Harris and Flores nodded and waved on their way out, and then I called, "Go get 'em, boys," at their backs, before they were gone out toward the city, where the new staging was already underway.

37

There were no MILES simulation systems on base in Kisufim. One was not made to endure the encumbrance of rows of black sensors that left him invincible everywhere else. In Kisufim we were no longer being given manufactured stresses to prepare us for real ones, though whether this amounted to a progression or a retreat was not easy to say.

Because in Kisufim one resembled less a grown lion on the open plain than a watchful turtle, limbs halfway in the shell and neck two-thirds. Here there were no forced marches kicking up conspicuous dust columns, no rowdy blanks fired at the sky, and no more running in the open air, because Kisufim excised a cost-prohibitive tax on each of these. There was simply no room for them in this tiny metal outpost, where we holed up and busied ourselves watching the clouds for signs of rain.

Kisufim allowed us no more running except the kind I knew from Be'eri, because all our *running toward* had been replaced with *running from*. Despite our conditioning, not all of us had yet known this form of running: the prey's form of running, one for which no amount of hunter's running toward can prepare. It is a higher form, as after all, any honest man who has done any real running from will report some loss of taste for running toward.

It is why no one who has been prey can regress in full to hunter, why no one who has come awake to running from can squander a remaining lifetime running straight toward. And I remember this image of our first alarm, a panoramic freeze-frame of these men discovering their limbs moving them for the first time, instead of the reverse. In the far distance, viewing this frame with the extravagant leisure we now possess, one sees the first black missile soaring on the horizon and its shadow stretching on the earth below, the two of them not to coincide near us, not this time. In the foreground, the alarms on the roofs and walls exploding at one satanic frequency, and all of us in our fullest, most organic motion, eyes wide with discovery like reborn children; too young for fear, just the ecstasy of birth, in a wordless mid-sprint senate, interrogating one another, hey, ain't this a thing.

All of us together in a lasting frame, one containing our common running at this higher form. Away from the missile and toward a truth of no regression: that only prey and not hunter can seek freedom, and that no one will seek freedom, or even know it, until he is made.

Today we made a grander image than in my first alarm at Be'eri, remembered for the calm with which we rose together in the living room and moved to the *merchav mugan*, the armored safe room, well in advance of the fifteenth second. There the walls were bare other than the paper drawings Dotan had taped along them, and we lay quiet other than the melody she hummed before the blasts began and until they ended, distant, just enough for little tremors in her paper drawings under strips of dried Scotch tape, which in this safe room sufficed to hold them, in this safe room where her humming was the loudest sound.

Dotan's humming as the missiles fell was not like the Sderot Haredi's prayer: hers was wordless, it was peaceful, and it was untrained. For these reasons or others, it was hers, not his, that remained with me in a place it made for itself rather than one I gave it. Soon after, I dreamed a *Tzeva Adom* in which the air was filled with soft, wordless humming, coming from a source I was running, running to try to find in time, awaking when I couldn't.

Today's *Tzeva Adom*, though, had no humming. It came in early morning and jarred most of us from sleep, and first I had my rifle in my hands and feet moving, then I determined this one was real, then I had the thought, on the run, of whether they would chalk me up differently if they got me here in tired *bet* rather than at Be'eri in a fresh white T-shirt, even though it was the same me.

But there was a difference: in Kisufim, running from was not just an instinct, but a duty, and here we were nearer the hunter, ten or twelve seconds rather than fifteen. It seemed a fair handicap for a trained combatant, and once we were all inside the shelter, past the popcorn of booms that did not come near us, not this time, after these I thought of Dotan and the paper drawings because I did not yet know she was safe; she was eight kilometers away. And so I had been right to think these would be the longest eight kilometers, but wrong to think their greatest length would be how far I was from Be'eri, instead of how far they were from me. And we emerged from the shelter to a resplendent desert sky, never farther from rain, and when I was able, I called Izzy, who confirmed the missiles had fallen far from them this morning and everyone was fine.

I went back to where the guys were hanging out in the shade outside the barracks, where there were posters and old sofas and we had touched it up like home. Now that we were on *kav*, which meant "line" and referred to the deployments done in rotation when Israel was not at war, we had broken distance with our commanders because there was simply no room for it either in Kisufim, and we had enjoyed dispensing with their veneer of invincibility, and they had enjoyed it even more than us, of course, and now they would brew Turkish coffee with us, sit on our sofas and play *shesh besh* (backgammon), share our cigarettes.

The sky still without a cloud, I sat on the stripped arm of a sofa and caught a mango from Nagosa, who had grabbed some extras from his kitchen shift, an act forbidden but never punished anymore. I peeled off half its skin and bit into it whole, and its juice ran sticky down my chin onto my shirt. Balkan Beat Box was playing through the speakers a couple guys had set up during our first week, and I was offered a cigarette and had to decline and explain I had never had one. I added that bit because I loved being offered cigarettes, loved that they would never stop offering me one the next time, loved that they assumed I might change my mind any new day.

These autumn afternoons were cool and tonight would be cold, so I remembered to go inside to pack up in advance. I was in a small team leaving base after dark for a *maarav* ("ambush"), a stakeout in a place where hostile movement was suspected. We would set up in a small patch of land at the border, and for the next seventy-two hours not leave, while we took turns sleeping and keeping watch on the land around us. Inside I decided to get some extra rest, too, before night came, and climbed onto my top bunk, took off my boots, and dropped them with a thud to the floor below. The Balkan Beat Box album was playing loud outside the bunks, but it never kept me from sleeping, and this and the voices and laughter outside would be a fine soundtrack to my dreams, till the moon came up and the day began.

Modeh ani l'fanecha, melech chai v'kayam . . .

So Shapira said to God upon waking in the lower bunk before we rose. Like Chaim's words at Michve Alon, except that Shapira's were not reborn in my mind as if its own, did not catch me in a blurry stretch between sleep and waking, because those had gone away some time ago. By now, I woke with no ambiguity, a clean and hard transition, and these words were not mine: they came from outside, and they came from below me, not above.

... *shehechezarta bi nishmati* ...

As a child, I had sung these same words out loud in the morning, before I knew what any of them meant. In later years, I came to sing them quietly, then to say them just in my heart, before they left me altogether, in the way we are told that human sacrifice became animal sacrifice, then loud prayer, then prayer in the heart, and then no prayer at all.

But it was a comfort to hear him say what I could not, so I listened to him finish at a steadfast whisper, soft enough I must have been the only one to hear him, lying above him in our beds before we laced our boots for the night ahead.

... *b'chemlah rabah emunatecha.*

38.

And there was evening and there was morning, in this order. The native dawn of the cycle is the feminine, restorative, nurturing night, which before giving way to unforgiving day, provides a time of anonymity and comfort within the womb. The morning prayer *Modeh Ani*, said before rising, praises God for this restoration, in faithfulness returning one's soul to him to confront a new day. And so I rose after Shapira ended the prayer, without a word so as not to replace his, or wake the others who stayed curled in their beds. We had been briefed already in the day so we came to the yard where we had set out our vests, and where the carrier hummed ready at the gates beyond.

And we were on our way, six of us in the carrier silent other than the crunching rocks beneath, to the open desert, where we would lie in wait at the wall that cut through it. Then we were there and I saw into Gaza for the first time, the faint streetlights and green minarets, and it was my turn to sleep but still I watched them glow awhile before I curled up like the others back on base, and closed my eyes.

Then came a nudge and I woke clean and hard to my surroundings, and my turn to guard. The sky was still black so I watched the land in green through my Lior, but before long, the gray horizon and first red daylight appeared, washing out the green. Once the greens blurred together, I switched to my Trijicon, whose vision was powered by its red fiber-optic strip that harvested the light of day. Within, it was still too dim to see and yet now was the time for highest guard, the most hazardous stretch of day: no longer night when we could see in green and thermal streaks, not yet full light of day. The ambiguous stretch between darkness and light, the muffled in-between.

And though the Jewish day begins with night, it is not a clean and hard transition, because there is this time of ambiguity, this muffled in-between. *Bein hashmashot* means "between the suns," and refers to the time after the sun has set but while its fading light still colors the sky. Since to be between the suns is to be in doubt whether it is day or night, the first day's end or next one's dawn, we honor the Sabbath for twenty-five hours, from Friday's sundown to Saturday's third night star.

And though *bein hashmashot* refers to dusk, we come between the same suns again at dawn. And a man came now, walking in the field, drawing closer to the wall, alone. I could scarcely see him in the dark and I longed for more light to fill my sight, but I watched his silhouette steady against the field, still alone. And through the markings in my sight, I could see he had come to the edge of the 300-meter buffer zone, within which we were to watch closely any man who came, and shoot any man who came armed.

Last week the snipers downed a man who came running at the wall armed and alone. We were sitting on the couches with the music on when the spotter who had been there told us about it, and he said the man came with a rifle out in front of him, back and forth across his chest, and ran straight at the wall instead of in the zigzags everyone knows to run in to make a harder target, and that even after the first bullet, he did not stop, but seemed to gain speed instead. It made sense, one of us said in response. The kind of man who runs straight at the wall is not the kind of man who stops after being hit with the first bullet. He was right, I thought as I listened, though my mind was on the sniper, exhaling all the way out and firing bullet number two.

And he crossed the line and my breath went still. His figure darker, larger with each step, and I waited for him to break into a sprint with his weapon but he had no barrel at his edge, and he drew closer, inside the buffer zone. His silhouette emerging clearer against the field, walking within this blurred expanse, alone between the suns.

But he was a farmer, I came to see as light arrived to my fiber-optic. He breached the buffer zone, but instead of running at the wall, he turned, walked in parallel, and as it came brighter, I saw him kneel at the edge of the field. Poking at the field with the thing he carried, which I squinted to see was a spade of some kind, before he kept on, a hundred and fifty meters out, walking on the edge. In the full daylight now and it was not what I was prepared for, because within the zone they had said to shoot a man who was armed but not said what to do with a man who farmed.

"Is he allowed to farm?" I murmured to my mate, who watched him, too, lying prone together in the barren soil.

"No. But don't shoot."

I was glad of that consensus, and finger off the trigger, I came to admire his garden in the morning light, because a grittier play than a knife in a gunfight was his, a spade in Gaza's live-fire zone. He gathered nothing before leaving, not today, which only promised us he intended, spade in hand, to return another. And even as the sun rose, I remained dogged by my mate's answer, which was in unsustainable tension with itself: not a statement of our law but a whispered admission of the cracks in it. What it did was leave three hundred meters under no one's jurisdiction, in an aching in-between, like we had drawn up in life scale at the range. Practiced to supreme intimacy, unconscious competence, till the body knows before the mind. It was why I felt it in my chest on his first step across three hundred, then each step heavier than the last, swallowing up the distance between him and me.

Alone running in the field between the lambs and the dogs, late Saturday afternoon. And in my mind I returned to the border, to lying still as he drew in. His subversive farming operation, I recalled, had been conducted in the blurry in-between both in time and in place: the hour after dawn, in the 300-meter buffer zone. This had to be why I was haunted by his image, the darkened figure I had prepared to strike down, spade in hand, the one who would return again to tend his field of no one's jurisdiction.

Now I was running in my own blurry in-between, in time and in place, the field where I loved to remain for so long as I could be. I turned again to face the guard dogs, the lambs behind me. The sun had struck the horizon, and now the light was dimming. Still, I kept running. The dogs had started barking but it was probably again just at the birds who flew free in the sky above—and whatever it was, I was free, too, to run a little longer, in the Sabbath's stolen hour, in the borrowed time left till morning's third star.

39.

Morning comes fast in the Negev. A man is far removed from the white stupor of the little cities created in his own image, awake again to the night. Without pollution to delude his vision, he finds the stars fast and in breathtaking number: three to signal dawn, and just as soon engulfing all the sky. The rapid dawn means a shorter spell between the suns, a more honest Shabbat, less time sheltered in the blurry in-between.

The sky was black within an hour and we lay out on the lawn outside the house, Arad and I, far enough for quiet, close enough to make it back inside the armored room in case of an alarm. Most Saturdays I took an early bedtime after running, but tonight Arad had asked to go stargazing, and we bundled up with blankets, my rifle behind two locks in my room, and snacked on a bag of Noga's cookies and pointed at the stars. Arad led the constellation hunt, since he had learned a whole trove of them in summer camp before school returned in the fall.

"Orion the hunter! My favorite." He held his pointer finger out above to trace the belt of three stars.

"There, I see him. So bright. For a long time he was my favorite, too."

"Who is your favorite now?"

"Do you know Lepus the hare?"

"Who?"

"Orion's prey, just below. The two bright ones beneath his feet are the hare's ears. Then trace around his body. See his legs running from Orion and his dogs?"

"I see the ears."

Arad searched his book and found Lepus in the back where a wide-eyed hare was drawn bounding for his life between the lines.

"He is about to be caught, see how close Orion's dog is?"

"They seem close, but there is an incredible distance between. Many light-years."

"Wow. Maybe Orion will never catch him then."

"We can pray."

"Imagine being hunted forever!" He brought his finger back above again to point the way.

"Better than hunting forever."

He said nothing back and I feared I had said too much, but when I looked over, he had found his favorite at the front of the book again, humming lightly as his finger traced from Orion's club to his feet, one inch away and closing in on two tall, terrorized ears in the night sky.

40.

Hinei ma tov uma naim, shevet achim gam yachad. Behold, how good and pleasant it is when brothers sit together in harmony.

A typical stretch on deployment goes 17/4, meaning seventeen days on the line, four days *bayit*, then return. It meant only one Shabbat in three was honored at home and the other two spent on the line, out where sacred and profane wore the same soiled fatigues, because an exception to the Sabbath's prohibition of labor is for action to protect life. Still, what sacredness remained we honored with more of ourselves, and we stayed long after dinner at the tables set for us on the yard, joining in *zemirot*, Shabbat table hymns.

Haben zona bachar b'chir. The son of a whore chose the infantry. *Hu y'shalem et ham'chir*. He will pay the price.

We had begun the secular *zemirot* now, and this one rhymed only in Hebrew and had a gravity that did not survive translation either, a favorite as we chugged down the grape juice and pounded the tables in chorus, voices howling into the night up past the alarms perched along the roofs on all sides of the yard.

Tonight felt even better because I had helped prepare this meal, an hour ago still on kitchen duty under Hadi, my favorite cook. Since we had two cooks, who switched turns, they got extravagant vacations to the tune of fourteen days *bayit* before fourteen back on. It was easy to tell who of the two cooks was on base and who back home because, unlike nearly any other cook in the army, Hadi cared. A Persian Jew forced from his combat role by a leg injury, he found his stride again in the kitchens, where he told me on my first shift under him that his mother did not raise him to serve bad food. He talked like this between the orders he gave, and in his kitchen I forgot he was not one of us soldiers, because although he had given up his rifle, it was clear he remembered it, and maybe missed it, too.

"Get the onions, *habibi*."

I diced with care as he hammered chicken pieces for schnitzel, and he was telling me about the beautiful trip he had taken up north with his girlfriend before returning to base. I had not spoken to a woman in a long while. Hard to get as a soldier, maybe harder to maintain. Just the two of them in a tent under a million stars in the sky, Hadi recounted, and his voice came again now to ask what happened, because I had started setting out metal trays for schnitzel and there was a blue mixed with the reds. A tray painted *chalav* (dairy) in blue, with the ones painted *basar* (meat) in blood red. A base violation, one I had not beheld before now.

The law of Kashrut forbids consumption of meat and dairy in the same meal, so we segregate, too, all utensils, which must be dedicated to one and not the other. The army enforced this separation unsparingly, kept *chalav* and *basar* far apart in blue and red camps so that neither even saw the other. Most of us did not bother with these rules at home but had no objection to them here, in the way that an unbeliever might scoff at a man who prays for him yet quietly stick around till the end of the prayer.

But here a blue was drowning deep in the reds and it was jarring to the eyes. "Is this *traif* now?" I asked as I extricated the blue.

"I'm a cook, not a rabbi. The reds will get over it."

I took the blue to return it to the others—but on the way I realized I had asked about the stray blue, but he had answered about the reds who saw it.

I turned to him, still holding the blue. "Is it to keep the red safe from the innocence of the blue?"

"What?"

Hadi had been back to blue now, I thought. But really he was in between, he was blending both, which as we knew was an intolerable condition, which might have been the hardest place of all.

"Is it more to protect the reds than the blues, to protect the reds from remembering?" I was sure he had answered the question already, now that I asked it.

"I think the reds have already forgotten it, *achi*, don't worry about details."

So I left the blue with all the others and before long forgot it, the smell of hot schnitzel filling the kitchen and soon everything was ready to serve. There were songs rising from outside so it seemed the scent had drawn the guys to the yard, and Hadi let me go so I exited to join them, seated with their rifles in their laps at the table, singing their songs of praise.

The goats and lambs bleating out together in harmony, feeding time at the Be'eri petting zoo before Shabbat, a pleasant time to join my father the groundskeeper puttering in his golf cart and making the rounds, the animals delighted to see us.

"What if *Tzeva Adom* comes here?"

"An alarm, or a rocket?"

He was right to clarify. I had asked the question in a blurry way, not to gain an answer so much as have it heard, in the way of a prayer. I had asked the same thing to Dotan earlier when we first visited the zoo, in the same muffled way so as not to corner her, and she pointed her little finger to the shelter nearby and I ended the inquiry for my own protection, as we went to see the next animals together. But I had little to protect from Izzy, and he even less from me, so I remembered to ask him, too, when I had him alone, but now he wanted a question and not a prayer.

"A rocket, I guess. Has one ever fallen here in the zoo?"

"No, not here. God has mercy on the animals."

It was not the answer I'd expected, because Izzy did not pray. But I had only started thinking it through when he added, "It's the same reason we don't have a synagogue on the kibbutz, since it would be the first place to be hit. At Be'eri nobody speaks the tongue of angels."

He got off the golf cart to open the next pen and walked in with the lambs while I stayed on board. These words of his included me now, too—they must have.

He went inside the shed, as though to leave me with what he had said, or rather as though solely with the aim to get his work finished. He was inside for a moment, and I took the time to imagine being in a synagogue when the alarm came, and I shivered, ran away back to the thought of being here behind the gate with the smiling lambs when her call sounded.

"What about an alarm then?" I asked as he emerged and locked the shed, which was only to guard its fruits from the lambs, forbidden to them for their own good. "What happens when you're here with the lambs and an alarm comes?"

"It is the most peaceful place on the kibbutz for an alarm. Her voice comes on and for all four calls they stay lying down eyes closed on the grass."

"What about you?"

"I run."

41.

June 2006, early morning on the border, between the suns, an ambush squad wove through the web of tunnels that spidered through the underground, dense cores and tangled lengths of roots to sustain them. Surfaced from the dark and blew open a tank's rear with a rocket-propelled grenade, gunned down two who tried to climb from the flames, and drew in closer to throw more grenades, because they knew a tank holds commander, driver, loader, and gunner.

Nineteen-year-old Gilad was asleep in his seat because it was not his shift, awakened to the missile's impact, to Commander Hanan and Driver Pavel climbing out of the wounded tank yelling at him to move, then gunfire and no more yells, and he froze in his gunner's seat, on which he had been trained. Then came explosions inside and he did not know where Roi the loader was but kept in his seat, where it was safer, till the smoke was spreading through the tank and he could not breathe, and he moved then, climbed out to the turret, leaving on the floor his M16, on which he had been trained. From the turret he saw a man climbing the front of the tank and right next to Gilad was the mounted .50-caliber machine gun, on which he had been trained—but he was frozen, Gilad later explained, seated for an interview. "I was completely confused. I did not think about anything." Gilad the gunner put up his hands without one bullet, and they closed in and seized him, took him under through the web of tunnels and held him five years in the dark.

On October 18, 2011, it was a Tuesday morning like most others. My dream last night had been beautiful, just us sitting outside the barracks, except the roofs had no alarms all along them, only speakers playing music. And the music was in Hebrew and our voices and my thoughts, too, without any English ones to get between me and the others.

I woke up before the morning flag ceremony, quiet on the yard, went to check the assignments chart, and it was an easy stretch ahead for me, too: just two guard shifts and a kitchen shift in the next few days before home, which was close enough to walk to, though instead I would always hop on the leaving army bus which passed Be'eri on the highway, and get off there at the roadside, wave at the guard, and walk through the yellow gate.

I went back to the bunks, where the other men were rising now, and we shined our shoes for the ceremony, and on the yard they raised the flag and it filled out in the wind. And when our company commander addressed us, he had a special air in his voice, because apart from our morning briefing he had more to say, because Gilad was coming home.

We had reached an agreement with Hamas on a prisoner exchange: one Gilad in exchange for one thousand twenty-seven of theirs, a mournfully, characteristically self-degrading ratio for Hamas to acquiesce to. Many serving life sentences, responsibility among them for lifetimes of terror, hundreds of dead. But across Israel's streets and highways were blue-and-white banners reading *Gilad Adayin Chai*, "Gilad Is Still Alive." And to us it did not matter he was no war hero, because on day one of basic we had more hero's blood in each of us, but by now, one year in, we had more of Gilad's.

Today he was coming home, and we crowded into the mess hall, which because it was the base's only concrete building, served also as our shelter, where we were safe. And inside we massed around a small television, and together we watched Gilad come home, and there were many of us and just one screen, and we watched them welcome Gilad, and their necks and arms were entangled with mine, and we watched Gilad find his father.

When I returned home to Be'eri on Friday, there were new blue-and-white banners strung across the lawn reading *Kama Tov Sh'bata Habaita, Gilad*, "How Good It Is That You Have Come Home, Gilad." And after I had cleaned up and locked away my rifle, there was a feast in the *cheder ochel*, and then live music and dancing out on the lawn. And the music was in Hebrew, and our voices and my thoughts, too. We stayed out late on the grounds that night, because we were so happy for Gilad, and because it was so good to have come home.

42.

At times I felt as though I were a toy soldier, or a chess piece, a man who did not choose the things he did but only saw them, passive, like a green plastic man who brandishes his rifle forever and keeps his little eyes opened in fright, or a wooden knight who is jumped and landed in places that go against reason.

In this passivity I found resentment, but then comfort, to think that only part of me would fire, and the other part would have nothing to do with it. In a five-man firing squad, one man receives a blank in his rifle, and maybe this blank was the difference between duty and murder. None of the men is told who has the blank, which means each man's rifle contains one-fifth of a blank. And if you asked any man after, he could tell you that to murder someone is to shoot them at one hundred percent, and he had shot at only eighty; that he did not choose any of these things, but only saw them. I was sure that I, too, would shoot at no more than eighty because I had come to understand the live rounds in my rifle were, at the least, one-fifth blank. In this passivity I found comfort, too.

I would turn these rounds over in my head and fingers, in the calm of loading magazines for the shift to come. But I put them off my mind once we were on the move, and tonight we had set out after dark again and it was cold, but warm beneath my vest, moving fast while crouched and between places of cover. We were not under fire but were prepared to be, at least in the sense that our helmets were on, and as we covered one another and stayed low moving toward the base, I was calm, because we were not under fire and because there were seventy-two hours still ahead of us, still to be seen.

The carrier had dropped us to the sand, loud engine vetoing our silence, then at last it was gone and we were alone in view of Marmorek, a base just up the border from ours, one that had been permanent until it was deserted. Now it was permanent in its desertion, or so I understood, because this base had been an important one in the region before intel came through that the tunnel roots were clawing, stretching themselves under, soon to sprout explosive charges in the earth beneath, and detonate. On receipt of the intel, the order was issued from all the way up the chain for Marmorek to be abandoned on short notice, not a fire drill evacuation but overnight or so, enough time to choose some of the things you do on the way out, instead of only see them.

For the next three nights and days, our team was to stake out in the old turret along Marmorek's western wall, which ran right upon the border, in anticipation of hostile movement across. After the carrier was gone and we had lain motionless awhile to detach ourselves from its loud wake, we had a clear night and bright moon, and began to come through the gates to the yard, one at a time under the others' cover. Inside, we found it empty but saw across in the moonlight, to the barracks and the bare flagpole alone in silver light at the center of the yard.

On command of our platoon leader, Ohad, the men made their way across the yard, one covered man at a time, to the turret at the west end. Ohad and I stayed back together, because as sharpshooter, my role was to enter the structure with him to secure it, ensure it was not occupied so we could turn our backs to it as we watched the border. Once the others were across, Ohad and I entered the building as trained, he first, because he was the officer and had been trained to say *acharai* ("after me") and intend it. My barrel over his shoulder and to the near side of the room as he went in and far, and our headlamps on, because inside there were no windows and no lights. In the first room it was dark with a trail of moonlight, but by the second it was whole blackness and our headlamps were strong, cutting white beams into the black, our necks gliding left and right to coat the room in white, to see what we needed.

In the hallway it was black. We were unwelcome with the rats who ran past our feet along the walls, and I was no longer calm as I had been on the way in. In the next room there were bunks in the dark, and my beam's edge hinted a crumpled figure, but when I turned to light it up, it was a couple of pillows and a shirt left tossed on the bed. On the floor were strewn trash and clothes because the departing men, like sailors on a sinking ship, were not moved to ensure it reached the bottom spotless. Then a bathroom, the stall doors open except one, so I went and kicked it in to be sure, and a mess of bats flew out clawing at my eyes, and when I shrieked, Ohad jumped in from the hall behind, but it was quiet then, bats settling their wings in the corners of the room, we standing in the center, all of us breathing to collect ourselves from the trauma we had done one another.

There were just a few more rooms to clear, so Ohad entered one and I another. More bunks, then under my white beam was a chess board with an unfinished game. Across the room a board sitting on one chair between two others, and then I was standing over it, looking down.

It was just a chess board with cheap plastic pieces; we had more rooms to clear, but now I was studying the board, then was in the game, because I had loved chess since I was a boy. White was on the attack, his men closing in, and I wondered whose move it was because this was always critical, but his position was so strong, it almost did not matter. Something was not right; there was a black knight in a place it should not have been. A position that could not have occurred in a game, because this lone knight was far behind the surging whites, jumped and landed in a place that went against reason.

I searched the field for a reason, a story for how he got there, before I caught myself, snapped back to the surrounding walls, which were black. I remembered where I was, and that I was afraid. And I brought my gaze and white beam up and away from the field, letting the dark swallow it again, and turned my rifle away from the men to leave them, black and white, undisturbed in their assault.

I found Ohad and we had cleared the building, so we emerged into the moonlight through the door we had first entered, and joined the others at the turret to begin our watch. Across the way we saw the lights in the houses and settled in to watch for movement, but in the time before it was my turn to sleep, my mind stayed on the board back inside. That position was impossible, so I was wrong to assume there had been two men in two chairs, the match unfolding when the call came like Vesuvius, their incomplete game immortalized. No, this board was in a state of completion, an art piece by a nameless man on his way out, for a nameless man who came in. And I shivered in the cold because I was no longer moving to stay warm. I looked back at the doorway, into the black where the knight waited—but snapped awake again, remembering my eyes had drifted from where they needed to be. And so I brought them back to where my scope still rested on the white lights across the border, and returned myself to watching them in green.

43.

Green crowns in the night. A new dawn on the border, at another point out in the open not far from the base we left behind, nor from Marmorek left behind before that. And lit up in green were the minarets in the town, near and bright, so I could see their green with my naked eye without painting them in the green of my Lior, which was a dull and washed-out green that made most things look the same. Tonight was warm and had a different feel than Marmorek, because this was not our first time lying on the border looking beyond, but was the closest we had been to the people who lived there. At our stretch of border tonight, the nearest homes were running right at the edge of three hundred, just at the far side of in-between.

Tonight there were green lights in the towers and yellow ones in the streets below, and music in the air. It must have been loud at its source to make it faintly to our ears out here, and I lay still in prone, but then a strange thing happened and my toes began to wiggle to its rhythm, ten of them up and down beneath my boots' rigid steel. I caught myself and stopped promptly, since it was neither safe to be dancing here on the border nor proper to do it to their music—and I looked over at the officer who led our team, prone and peering over the border, and sure enough, his feet were stone-still so I made mine the same.

Across the border they had to be celebrating something but I knew not what, and they surely did not know we were here because we had not been invited and could have cramped the mood. And this music was not for us, but we had nothing else to do for the next hours so my toes began itching to wiggle again. I wondered if it might not be too much to ask to permit myself to enjoy the music while we waited, and then wondered if our officer would permit it, too, if I were to ask.

But if I was permitted to enjoy the music, then I wondered if I could not make believe we were part of this celebration, too. I knew this asked too much, so instead I imagined a more foolish me that I could regress to and who would believe this, in the way that a child born on June 14, Flag Day, might walk about on his birthday and see bright flags waving on the porches and love his neighbors for celebrating him, and go on this way until some unwelcome day came and he came to love them less.

And so for this reason I wished not to know what they celebrated, because it could risk making me stop wiggling my toes like my officer presumably had done long ago. I looked at him again, stone-still from his toes up to his right eye, which rested in his scope watching the city in dull green despite the bright lights, and I wondered if to be an officer is to swear off wiggling your toes forever.

But I would never be an officer, because I had only a month left to serve. And this made me happy and sad at the same time, sort of like the way it felt to lie here with the brothers I loved and protect the family I loved who were sleeping not far from here; none of us speaking, but all of us seeing the music and the firecrackers on the earth, and the fires in the sky.

44.

Jeep speeding over the earth, like our first trip to the border but no more groans from the rocks beneath, just the smooth whipping that comes from below a jeep that does not roll but flies, wheels too busy to spend any time in the spaces between.

Then off the rocks and north on the highway, the one that took me home from base to Be'eri, and the yellow gate was just minutes away but now we braked for a hard right instead, to the gate of Re'im. Re'im was the kibbutz just south of Be'eri, whose name meant "friends," and I had met a couple of Arad's friends from here but not been before, now through the gates, rifles drawn ready for the next call.

The women who were our eyes on the walls, watching remotely from the cameras that ran all along, had spotted two armed men emerge on our side at dawn, headed for here. Today I was in *kitat konenut*, the alert team that sleeps with its boots on, first responders in scenarios like these. And we made it to Re'im ready to jump, but then the radio said we had lost their trace. No more visual, which probably meant they had scurried back under the web from which they'd come.

And so the tracks were cold, but not yet dead, and we were to stay here till the hunt was through. So we unbuckled our helmets and stayed at the rim of the kibbutz instead of going in, because although the children of Re'im were more accustomed to the sight of *bet* than those of Tel Aviv, *bet* was still a thing no one, not even a child, should be made to see without reason.

Except the sheep, the incorrigible sheep, there in the pasture beyond Re'im's houses and within its barbed wire, where the rockets never fell. A trove of them idle on the grass, stares even more cottony than the ones at Be'eri's zoo, where a gated spectacle was made of their innocence, where here it was their untarnished condition instead. I was glad to see them, too, or rather to be seen by them, unconditionally in my nakedness, like one feels to unclothe in front of a loyal pet who never fell from Eden and who sees you just the same. And so we sat with them in our Eden, our man-made green bastion at the edge of the unkept desert, for as long as we had left, sun dawning over the horizon now and filling through the dunes in gold.

It could be a while until the call for *chazara l'shigra*, "return to routine," which would take us back down the highway, obeying the speed limit, from our green bastion to the gray base. So in the space between, in the peacefulness left to us before the end of the alert, cigarettes were passed around and the Turkish coffeepot brought out, because the driver kept one ready in the trunk for scenarios like these.

"I wonder if these two were released for Gilad," Commander Tal posed, lying back with his elbows in the green. Two sheep drew in to where we had spread in a stray formation in the pasture, weapons shed to the tall grass, one nuzzling on the edge of Tal's rifle where he'd set it down. He petted its head while it licked the barrel, other hand on his lit cigarette.

"Could be Operation Cast Lead all over again soon," thought Barkan, not in answer to Tal's musing but in addition to it, the only way he was able. Barkan, who had shared his food with me in war week, and carried me, too, as I learned from Oren after I woke up. I wanted to share this with him now also, but was finding I could not, not the way I wanted, because my release loomed in a couple weeks. I had tried to forget it was nearing, but then reminders started coming from my men, first weekly and soon daily, by saying things like these.

So I only nodded, because that was a thing neither one of us could know, but which only he was carrying. The coffee was done brewing now and I took a small cup, careful not to pour more than the others would get in turn. I was offered a cigarette again, too, and passed like the times before, and hoped they would not stop asking tomorrow, or the day after.

Out beyond the barbed wire, the day's first public buses were passing on the highway, sun almost all the way up now, eyes and lenses sharpening at the edge of the blurred zone. Even after the sun had risen to the sky, it was quiet for what seemed a long while before we were pulled back awake by the call, *return to routine*, on the jeep radio, which we had turned all the way up, to permit ourselves in the meantime to sit farthest out on the grass, to place ourselves at the greatest distance between.

45.

I remember the cold morning it occurred to me that I was not going to die. Autumn had come to winter, and in my final week I stood guard alone in the south tower, our flag resolute above me, sun rising and my men stirring in the barracks across the way below. One of them, just back to base from a few nights on the border, stumbled out toward the shower room, filthy and naked but for a dusty towel on his waist.

It was Oren, who had carried me. His rifle clacked against his bare back, hanging on a strap that from a distance I could see was still damp from the night, from the way it gripped his skin. I pitied him—then shuddered at what I had just done.

For one heroic second I tried to unfeel the pity; insisted into the air that I carried no more assurances than him, than any of them. That today could be it. A grotesque idealism, but I clung to it sweetly. Yet the fight had slunk away from me even before Oren reached the shower room door, because Oren had twenty months to go and I, five days. And then the truth that had forced its way through was all I could see: I would leave, and each one of my men would load his rifle again the next morning.

Oren entered the shower room below, and I knew that from inside he would sing, as he always did no matter how cold the water. And I turned away, because I did not want to hear it. I stared south out from the tower into the empty gray morning, held my gaze firm into nothing even as I now faintly heard the water start to strike the concrete, and the caged bird begin its song.

46

June under the heat of summer, and we had only just arrived at our new base in Hebron. Early morning before climbing the guard tower for my shift, I stopped to piss on the perimeter wall at the foot of the tower. There I spotted something behind the tower, wedged between tower and wall: a crumpled flag, trapped in the tight gap between them. I leaned all the way into the gap and fished out the flag with the tip of my rifle, then hands.

The shredded flag must have fallen from its perch atop the tower. The army destroys fallen flags, so this one had to have slipped from the pole without notice. I stuffed it into my pack and hurried up the tower stairs so I would not be late to replace the man still standing guard above.

After finishing my shift, I returned to the barracks to unfurl the flag. I did not know how long it had been trapped behind the tower, but I opened it to find scarcely more than half a flag, shorn diagonally across its center just above the tip of the star. The cut was ragged and the white browned and brittle with dirt. I bunched it up again and stashed it in my bag for home, eager to drape it on the bare wall in my room at Be'eri. It would be my room's sole decoration other than the handmade scroll given me by Avi's mother, a renowned Jewish artist, reading "Every Journey Brings Blessings." The scroll sat unrolled so its words read along the length of the sill of the window, through which I would sit on my bed and watch the chickens cluck in the morning, and now I would hang this flag above, with reverence, not unlike the way Avi hung the flag in his room.

But I stopped, because this felt like theft—I needed to hear someone tell me I could keep it, too. There was at least one commander I thought would say yes, so I went to find him.

I asked around for him and found him on a cigarette break, and brought him the tattered flag, which I had hidden in my bag on the way so I would not have to get more than one yes. He spread it open before him with both hands, and one of its corners frayed off in his fingers as it stretched. He brought his eyes up to me, over the flag between us.

"You want this thing? You know you can have a new one at the bus station for thirty shekels."

"Yes, I want this one much more."

He gave it another look, shrugged, and I was glad I had chosen him to ask.

"Of course you can keep it." He stretched the flag out wide again, to fold what remained of it into dignified quarters. He finished smoothing its corners, and pressed it back into my hands. "As long as you do not disrespect it."

47.

The colossal flag soared high over the Western Wall, engorged in the wind, its whites resplendent against the orange sky. We stood below in the square, facing the Wall as one, shoulder to shoulder, rank and file. It was winter in the Old City, and our anthem flooded through the square and echoed from the Wall itself, as the square pulsed and overflowed with our loved ones come to witness our induction into the force.

Then a suspended moment, a space in which the ancient Wall loomed, our anthem throbbed, the white lights came alive, and our flag more brilliant still against the fading sky. The space stretched and swallowed, and in our rows we were as captives within it. And I stood, and we stood, and our backs now stiffened at our brigade general's ascent to the stage. He began to speak, but his register was lofty, above what I had yet attained in these first weeks, so I let his words sound instead as hymn, reading his face, and his eyes, matching the cadence of his baritone to the swelling and snapping of the flag above.

He completed his address, and each of our commanders now marched into place at the head of his unit. Beside each commander was a black tower of M16s, each weapon waiting to be entrusted to new hands. Four walls to each tower's architecture, a log cabin of massed firepower: each weapon a layer, resting its barrel on the shoulder of the one beneath it, and lending its own shoulder to support the barrel above, an undamaged symmetry to their formation. In front of the commander was a table, atop it the book, its text facing forward for the eyes of each initiate, who would be called to lay his palm upon it and swear on its contents to honor the weapon he would receive.

One by one, each soldier from the ranks was called to accept his weapon. As my turn drew near and my pulse rose to a hammer, I found calm in the posture of our general, who looked over us from on high. I prepared to step forth to my commander and the Wall, and my palms opened and swelled. Then I found in them the black metal of the M16 he had pressed on me—and I held fast. I returned to my ranks and there, like the soldier beside me, took up drill position, lower length of my rifle resting in my right hand, left hand across my body to secure it as it looked skyward. Soon the last of us had accepted his weapon, and our formation stood ready.

"*Ani nishbah! Ani nishbah! Ani nishbah!* (I swear! I swear! I swear!)" The vow thundered through us with the force of ages, one single breath expelled from the hewn stone to the Jerusalem sky. My hands locked around my weapon, the throngs erupting in affirmation of our vow, and I carried not the weight but only the splendor of our charge. I felt brave, and I felt safe. This was a special night, because ever to feel both in the same breath was a rare and precious thing.

What vow had I taken, after all? I awoke in my top bunk on the last day, and would be honorably discharged—but had I been faithful to my vow? If I was not now breaking it, then had it only ever been so fickle? So muffled and small? Better to have taken and fulfilled a weak vow, or taken and run from a brave one?

I awoke from these dreams to find my rifle under my pillow for the last time. Our divorce was already underway, because the day I stood in the tower listening to Oren's song, I was relieved of two futures: that I would die holding the rifle or that another would through my sight. These were two visions, but they were born and ran together, and died together, too.

The rifle felt foreign now, a prop I carried without knowing why. But it was steady even as it disentangled from me, and I came to hold it with an awe like I remembered from its first days in my arms. No longer an extension of them, it took on new elegance, new curves to its body and sensations in its smooth metal. It gleamed like the first day, brimming with a force I had borrowed but was never mine. A force that flooded my veins when we stood under the Wall, and was slipping now in quiet, returning.

After rising, I hung it from a hook on the barracks wall, and stood back with two hands behind me, like Eli had done when we watched Shachar in the hall. I held up a camera to preserve the image of my rifle on the wall, then returned to my bunk to cradle it in my arms until the hour I was to report to the depot to surrender it. I arrived at the depot, stripped my rifle from my back, and handed it to the attendant, and my weapon resumed its position among the racks of others like it. I saw it then within a black tower in front of the Wall, and nearby a new, trembling pair of hands. I gave it one more look on the rack, my last chance to distinguish it from any other M4A1 carbine of the same make and manufacture, and walked off the base.

I was honorably discharged on December 29, 2011, with the rank of Corporal. My discharge papers' *ha'aracha* ("appraisal"), upon which was stamped the seal of the Israel Defense Forces, stated of me in full: "Executed his charge to the satisfaction of his commanders' will."

48.

Be'eri's oranges were now in their fullest season, and we sat out eating baskets of them. Shabbat, my parents threw me one more *al-ha-aish* before my flight on *Yom Rishon* in the morning. As we ate, it felt untrue having been accorded that recognition—"executed his charge,' in ink already dried—sitting here this evening in a place chosen near enough to the house to make it to the armored safe room, if we needed.

But right now the air was still. And full, and rested. The radio's meter-long antenna was tuned to the army's station, *Galgalatz*, the only broadcast that reached us in the Negev. They mostly played Israeli pop and rock, but always cut it instantly for emergency announcements, just as fast as the kibbutz alarms sounded. Which meant that music on *Galgalatz* was proof that all was calm, at present.

And the music played. *You and I, we'll change the world.* Arik Einstein's classic. *You and I, we'll try from the beginning*, floated Arik's clear, gentle voice across our patio—and until now, I had never so admired his conviction, or how much he was holding up, holding down, in holding to it. As he held us through his chorus, I remember that I somehow knew for certain: Arik would not permit a soul to interrupt him. Not before he had finished, and we had heard him.

It was otherwise a quiet dinner, not least because Izzy's chicken skewers were exquisite. After Arik finished as he had promised, the broadcast faded to a routine top-of-the-hour news minute. We wrapped up slowly and stayed out awhile for tea, even after it was dark and *Yom Rishon* was upon us.

I promised I would be back to visit, the kids went to bed for school tomorrow, and I, too, climbed the stairs to finish packing.

"*T'nadned oti* (Push me)!" Dotan had called again, earlier this afternoon on the swing set. She knew that I was leaving in the morning. Even so, when she flew higher on the swing and laughed, I could hear no difference in it.

I had no rifle behind two locks in my room, no *aleph* laid out on the floor to rise and don in the morning. And in this way, to leave the army was hard, but after that was done, I found that leaving Be'eri was easy. Be'eri had been home only so long as I had an army bus to board again on *Yom Rishon*, so Be'eri was not a place I could stay, not if I would only live here, and not defend it.

And of course, there was no peace. Not before the redemption of the color red for Dotan, nor before the exorcism of Baruch's tortured ghost over the city of Hebron. You come to know the names of these ghosts, you walk the paths where they glide and cast their shadow, you carry them, too, within yourself—yet for it all, they are no friendlier. And as I was not an exorcist, nor a peacemaker, nor even a citizen of Israel, I packed up my half a flag, my discharge papers, and the things I had long ago brought from my home, and left to seek and pursue peace of my own.

PART IV

There are five matters in our world which are one-sixtieth of their most extreme manifestations. They are: fire, honey, Shabbat, sleep, and a dream. Our fire is one-sixtieth of the fire of purgatory; honey is one-sixtieth of manna; Shabbat is one-sixtieth of the World-to-Come; sleep is one-sixtieth of death; and a dream is one-sixtieth of prophecy.

—Talmud Tractate Berachot 57

49.

*N*eshek, the Hebrew word for "weapon," is a product of the same root as the word *neshika*, "kiss." The two are attached at the hip, a mere molecular twist apart. When I discovered this twinning in the thralls of basic, it was perverse to the ear—but by the time I had surrendered my rifle, it was an unvarnished truth.

After my rifle was gone, I grasped for it. Mornings, in the womb before waking, eyes folded to the world, I would lay my hands on the rifle beside me, then claw blind for it when it was not there. Even gone, it remained the point of entry to consciousness, governed the way I was born each day, the way my eyes came open, and what they remembered as I rose.

The waking world, too, was colored by its loss. Where I walked, a phantom rifle hung from my shoulders, its gentle knock against my back at every step. In rising to my feet a reluctant buoyancy, an artificial lightness to my frame. And it was true that I was lighter now, and that I did not want the rifle back, or to see it again. But I wanted to hold it in my arms just one more time.

At LAX, the customs officer took me to the side room after hearing me explain the nature of my trip, because he wished to know if I had renounced my citizenship. I told him with imperfect confidence that I had not, and repeated what felt like the most convincing thing to say, which was that American citizenship was still the only kind I ever had. He seemed invested in a different answer, said he would consult his superiors, and picked up the phone while I sat in the chair still wearing my army boots without more to say in my defense. I watched his white chins quiver righteously as he spoke into the receiver louder than was warranted, and it occurred to me his stiff blue uniform was an *aleph* that had not in all its days seen a *bet*. He went on in what appeared less an effort to describe my disloyalties to his superior than to me, and I grew unsure whether there was anyone on the line—but after some time he was answered from above and said I could pass, which was like being offered admission into heaven yet suddenly finding the air quite nice outside it. Hesitant to concede I wanted passage through any gate of which he was keeper, but my parents were waiting so I got on my way. I had not much else to carry with me, just what I had packed from my room in Be'eri, and though I had missed the first bus while he detained me, I was able to board the next without further controversy, headed for home.

Back in the house of my childhood with Mom, I ate everything she cooked but made time, too, to stop at all the restaurants, whose online menus I had browsed from internet cafés in Israel to see what the specials were. Now I ate each place's specials and my old favorites, too, gained back nine pounds in my first two weeks. And at the end of these two weeks, too, came my appointment at the clinic, to get checked for post-traumatic stress disorder. Not because I thought it urgent, but because it was a check under the hood I thought a soldier was supposed to get whenever he stops being one, whenever he reenters orbit.

I was declared free of the syndrome, and though I was no psychiatrist, it made enough sense. I had no horrors by night, no shocks by day, none of these things I had heard beset real soldiers coming home from real wars. My pain was one of the heart, and though it throbbed there, it had not metastasized to take over my lungs or brain. My pain ached but would not shoot searing down my limbs, not ambush in places it did not belong. I was free to go fall in love or chase paychecks without the tinnitus of war chasing me into the office, free to remember my lessons but not be drowned by them, traumas in some concentration lesser than one that makes a poison.

In a certain manner, the closest I had ever been to a real war was with that hideous black-notched Vietnam M16 at Michve Alon, sweating onto it under the sun the first day it fell into my hands, that very first time I felt something like a soldier. And driving home now from the clinic, I thought again of the M16 and the man who held it before me, cradled it in his arms as he hopped off the carrier onto the sand in a strange land, clutching the rifle close because that's what he had. And I did not know his name, if he still lived today or if he had come home at all, and I had not before found a reason to shed tears for him, but I did now. And I let these two streams run free, collect in clear stains that would soon dry without a trace on my new blue jeans, let these streams flow, for him, as I kept two hands on the steering wheel, Bob Seger's "Against the Wind" on the radio, my clean bill of health riding shotgun beside me, the two of us almost home.

50.

I was free now, entitled not just to live my life as I wished, but to *keep* it. This, the latter right now seemed the surest difference between soldier and citizen. To be sure, a citizen's profession may impose myriad restrictions or even hazards to his life—but only the soldier waives the lawful right to *have* his. Soldierhood, at bottom, is a candidacy for death on behalf of the citizen, to whom he has allowed a mortgage on his very breath. (Hence, a soldier's death in action, though it is many things, is first a foreclosure by the citizen.) And apart from what hardships he may endure in his service, one who makes it out finds a fresh bewilderment: the disorientation of finding oneself holder and not debtor on this mortgage, the daylight of the sudden expungement of this lien on his existence.

As it happened, the doctor's stamp of mental soundness gave me a kind of permission, perhaps one I had sought, to continue in my reveries and rewinds and to feel them fully. Now that I was a citizen—that is, a man returned his life's full possession—this was an unhurried spring season. For the time, the hardest adaptation, the one that continued to arrive unexpected, was to awake without a weapon.

Winter in the Negev, before my M16 had even had an exotic M4A1 replace it. A classroom series on the field skills of basic training, such as the tourniquet and knots of other design. We rotated from room to room for our lessons, and in each room we laid down our weapons just for the moment, to free our hands for instruction. I had just finished a class and begun moving to the next, when a sharp static struck through my spine as I realized I was naked, had been naked since the first class in the circuit. I took flight back to the first room, where I knew I had left my rifle—and a commander was sitting over it, alone in the room, waiting for me.

Among the more contemptible atrocities a *Tzahal* soldier may commit is the misplacement of his weapon. The act is called *hafkarat neshek*, translating not merely as forgetting one's weapon but forsaking it. The commander rose from his chair and stood over my rifle, towering over me though he stood five foot nine, and I knew as I met eyes with him that I was fucked. I expected no leniency, and for my offense I would receive the punishment of "Shabbat," which seemed a strange name for this punishment, to name the punishment the thing that is taken from you. It meant that the next time I would otherwise have a weekend reprieve off base, I would instead be taken to the edge of the yard to watch the buses leave.

I knew that when *hafkarat neshek* became a repeat offense, it could carry escalating punishments. But I would not forsake my rifle again, because I was learning my lesson now, tonight, without the redundant weekend to follow. Now, static still jumping to my fingertips, I stepped into the room as lamb to an altar, would not speak unless spoken to. And my commander did not speak. He handed me my rifle, and walked out of the room. I watched him step into the night, then I looked back down at my rifle to find I had already brought it in to hold against my chest. My heart began to settle, my oxytocin to swirl. There was such peace in having it back in my arms.

51.

The nonlinear and weaving ways of grief, was how a teacher once had said it. It was a finely chosen pair of words, the first recalling shape, the second texture. The griever as a kind of blind, determined artist, *weaving*, present progressive tense, in a long, unfinished act of his creation. Grief, without question, was the name for it: for my men in Kisufim, for my family down the road from them. This much was sure, if only because it was so specific, so precisely woven, when I happened back upon the places I had made for them.

Tonight, for instance, we were sitting for a Friday movie just like always, on the living room projector. Dad had picked out *Some Like It Hot*, the Marilyn Monroe comedy. We sat back, dimmed the lights—and there in front of us were Joe and Jerry dressed up and on the run, trying to piece it all together and stay alive while at it.

"Yesh chamim v'taim."

Ziv whispered on the radio and was gone, with godlike concision. The rest was commentary.

"Did he say *chamim v'taim*?"

Chamim v'taim meant "hot and tasty." In the field, it was our name for the rare event of any warm meal that was not boxed tuna rations. Ziv was more concise with his good news than his bad, and this announcement was his briefest of the day, but for now we kept our eyes on the fence, dreaming of lunch but not done earning it.

Today Shmuel and I held a post together, one of many along the West Bank barrier near the village of Shekef. We had drawn the day shift, 7 a.m. to 7 p.m., also welcome news, because tonight we would sleep while the others guarded by moonlight and the yellow glow of the lampposts that ran along the fence. And I doubted they were sleeping now anyway, in the room with the air conditioner that rattled and wheezed like the little engine that almost could.

When Shmuel and I were on our own, we talked mostly in English, about things we had left behind. "Did you know *Chamim V'taim* is also the name they use for *Some Like It Hot*? The Marilyn Monroe movie?"

"No, I had no idea," I admitted. Strange, because "hot and tasty" was not even a mistranslation but so far off as to be deliberate, as if chosen as a more honest way to say what the Americans had euphemized.

"Doesn't everyone like it hot?" I squinted back as the sun blasted and sweat collected at the corners of my eyelids.

"Yeah. Seems that way."

Between the two of us, Shmuel had more figured out, more calm in the spaces between—so I liked reminders like this one that he, too, was just going by what he felt, what he saw. And now what we saw was the delivery jeep stirring up dust on the path toward us, and we turned to catch the packs tossed to us by the soldier sitting in the back, the driver slowing to make his mate's throw easier, then gassing it for the next post.

We were delighted to find warm schnitzel and rice in the packs, and sat with our eyes back to the fence. Breaches were common on this stretch, and twenty meters down from our post was a fresh hole not yet patched from a break of a day before. A red flannel shirt still clung to the barbed wire where it had caught and been stripped off in the escape, and another roll of wire had been placed in front for now, till things could be made whole.

"I feel like the damn *migra* (US Border Patrol)," I said,

watching the shredded shirt hang limp on the wire, wondering where its owner was, while it fluttered now and then in the wind.

But Shmuel did not comment because he had spotted a truck rolling down a hill several hundred meters out, and I reported on the radio as it neared. I put down the schnitzel and raised my scope, and through it were five men standing in the bed of the truck as it circled looking for a soft spot at which to unload them. The second thing to do was turn around and look for another vehicle syncing movement on the highway, on our side of the barrier. The way to breach the fence was on foot, but the best escape once across was on wheels, and hence arose an industry, like Uber for the West Bank. But for now no car was behind us, and I turned back to Shmuel, who still held his scope on the circling truck.

"Five at a time?" he inquired to the truck, but also loud enough for me to hear it.

"Probably cheaper for each of them. They have to eat, too," finishing my last bite of schnitzel and returning my lens to the truck, which climbed back over the hill and out of sight, the mouse sure to try again when the cat was dozing, sure to find a better spot to make its play.

After lunch came a new radio call, assigning me to patrol up and down the length with another mate, Ofri, who was on his way here from the next post down. Ofri then arrived and, like the jeep, slowed but did not stop as I hopped down from the post to join him in stride, leaving Shmuel still peering through his scope for a trace of the vanished truck.

"*Hu m'chapes mashehu* (Is he looking for something)?" Ofri spoke no English so it was time to stop talking about things I had left behind.

"*Haya lanu eizeh achbar sh'barach* (We had a mouse that ran away)."

He was moving at a strong clip so I hurried to his side and

the sweaty insides of my thighs rubbed against my uniform's fabric, which would start to chafe them if we kept this rate. On our marches I would smack them with a protective coat of Johnson's baby powder, which a friend had given me to keep in my pack in an English-labeled bottle—but today I was without it, so I hoped Ofri would tire and slow his pace without my asking him to.

"How was the schnitzel?"

"Awesome."

All the talk either of us needed, because I was fine and he was fine and beyond that one does not talk during a movie. And we kept up under the sun and the men at the next post waved as we passed, and on the next stretch we passed a group of Arab laborers making additions to the fence. There was an irony in Israel hiring Arabs to strengthen the West Bank barrier, but one the parties were willing to overlook for business. But not all business partners are friends, and as we began to pass, one dropped a hammer and, while bending down for it, dropped his pants, too, and pointed his bare ass at us, to the high thrills of his peers.

I laughed, too, at his white ass in the sun, but cut it when Ofri snarled. "Dogs," he spat at the ground. "Their brothers murder our families, and so they get work helping build a fence to keep the animals out of our yard. And now they stand here and insult us."

And I was done—done with any laughs or any thought except to get us going, because even though there was everything to see here, there was also nothing at all. I marched away from where he had stopped, knowing he would catch up, sure enough now hearing his breath behind me, rifle back and forth across his chest, the two of us moving on fast to the next post, past the men who stood in a circle still laughing at our backs.

52.

Thirty seconds, touch the wall, return. A *Tzahal* soldier's most common orders are variations on a theme: run to a distant object, touch it, return to origin before it is deemed too late. The order is easy to follow and instills core truths from a young age, subjecting him to a form of forcible fetch in which he brings back nothing and is thereby unburdened of the illusion of intrinsic purpose. A soldier grows so accustomed to this form of order that what we say of one who has completed half his service and has half left is that he has "touched the wall." A big day for any soldier, one who has begun his way home. One who has spent the junior part of his service with fresh legs running toward, and enters the senior part with clear eyes, running from.

On a day in May 2011 that I do not recall, I touched the wall to no fanfare at all (seven months in, seven to go). It was in April 2012, after my release, that my mates touched the wall all at once, eighteen months in, same to go. They roasted a whole lamb on an open flame, given in tithe by the farm of Barkan's father for the occasion. It struck me as the ultimate act of red *basar*, the negation of blue *chalav*, to impale a young animal, specifically a lamb, and ritually consume it head to tail until no trace remained, chanting hymns round the fire to their barbarism, the attainment of their most euphoric reaches from anything soft or humane, the consummation of their running toward. A special day for me, too, seeing footage on Facebook from across the ocean a couple weeks later, once the men had next been allowed off base. On that day I watched their dark pixelated faces and heard their voices through my speakers in the songs I knew, on replay till I had sung along enough, and went to bed content to realize the lamb was already two weeks gone, and my boys already on their way home.

53.

My hands in the spring were already so soft. On their backs bronze to white, and on their palms, thick callus to unspoiled skin. Losing the hands that held my rifle's memory, fading to fleshy white whether I clenched my fists against it or otherwise.

It was around this time I decided to study massage. I enrolled at a local school in a night course including a survey of techniques, and on our first day it was advised that after completing our basic training, many of us might begin advanced training in methods like aromatherapy, deep tissue, or more esoteric schools like Rolfing or Shiatsu. I was put off by the idea of an "advanced training" and sensed I had not come to make a career—yet was enamored of this world, studied my textbook obsessively, scribbled sharp notes on the diagrams of the human heads and torsos.

Our leader, Jeanette, was a walking effleurage, and where she went, lavender followed. On day one she shook my hand with both palms, coating it in a lotion that seemed their natural secretion; quieted the nature calls trickling from the speakers, sat us in a crescent, and invited our inner children to sit, too. Then she stood and caressed the naked mannequin before us in demonstration, giving her eyes to each of us in turn, attentive to our comprehension and comfort. And surely a crack in her act, a single grain of irony would appear along the way, so I studied her for it, in her eyes, where I imagined she would first show herself—but they stayed blameless, and I adored her.

Her lesson ran through the first half of each class, and in the second we moved to the tables in the next room, formed pairs at each table, and alternated weaving our hands on one another's bodies. I delighted in lying nude on the table, rubbed by eager hands, the inert object of their discovery. And delighted in their amateurism, their finding their way in the dark over my joints and fibers, tripping and tumbling over my skin. Now and then Jeanette would glide by, advise a shift in technique, and demonstrate. The novice hands came away and in their place perfected strokes, no crevice a secret to them, finishing with a flourish before the clumsy ones' return. I welcomed them back, because Jeanette's hands had no need of me, but these did. Repurposed to warm mannequin, I wished to dedicate myself to science and lie here forever.

But in our changing roles it was not receiving but giving that was the reason I returned. Rediscovering the fasciae of the book diagrams, retracing Jeanette's circuits on the mannequin. My hands grew to relish a deep knot's release, delight carnally in running over thick tendons, revel in a premeditated thumbstroke to the occiput and the tremor after. Emboldened to uncover more Vitruvian secrets, more sleights to embed in my palms. There was force in my hands. It would well up as I buried them in two limbs, surge as I amassed the tension and released it, shuddering, end to end. It was a crackling, primal energy I had tapped, and wielding it had become my obsession.

On the last night I was paired with Ata, a Turkish ziggurat of a man with granite slabs for shoulders, so much surface area, I expended twice the lotion on him as on other classmates— but then twice the terrain to survey. First he lay on the table and I carved my hands into the ropes of muscle along his spine, cradling the life in his tissues and rearranging it, running knuckles down the iron tendons in his neck, studying his pulse as it thudded from behind them. Then I became his study, and

219

his boulder-hands made his touch unforgiving, amplifying the weight of their imprecisions—but when Jeanette's little hands replaced his in flawless form, I waited for the boulders' return.

Class ended then, chased out into the night by the trickling streams from the speakers behind. My head swam from Ata's unsubtle concluding experiments with a new cranial technique, my body's whole length greased with the lotion he had slid across. Temples throbbed under the white streetlights, palms slicked and oily—but this lotion was my own, from the grooves I had carved into Ata's spine before he turned upon mine. I made it to my car and stopped to view my palms under the light, larger than Jeanette's but secreting the same buttery film. Got into my car with the lavender air freshener that hung from the rearview, still dizzy so I reclined the seat, turned the key halfway to ignition and my speakers up high, to return to my senses before attempting to make the drive home.

54.

In late spring came a dream in which I returned to the sacred field of Be'eri. As ever, alone there in my time of late afternoon. Felt my feet on the cracked earth, and knew where I was, before opening my eyes to find the earth, lifting them to where the orange trees appeared, and behind them the barbed wire. For a time I was still, and breathed in the yellow that shone on the earth, in the trees, and in the wire and the sky beyond. Then, I felt that it was time to run.

I began to race across the field, west and east across its length, toward the setting sun and away from it, at my back. Though unencumbered, I felt exertion in each stride, and soon my feet grew heavy, vision unsteady, and I came to pant and gasp, each step heavier than the last till my chest pounded, head spun, hands fell to knees. I hunched over the ground, shoulders stooped, feet cemented in the earth. My chest heaved and throat clutched for air, and now one ragged, pained breath filled my lungs, my body folding into itself and into the earth. I heaved a second time, and now on my shoulders came the orange sun from the west behind. This second breath now filled me with lightness, rich and redeeming. With this breath I rose, limbs free, turning back to the west, able now to stare straight into the sun. I kept my gaze straight and my feet sped freely over the earth leaping and bounding, westward toward the end of the field even as the barbed wire beyond began to blur into the horizon.

55.

By June the last traces of my callus had been gone awhile. Today was the fourteenth, Flag Day, which was my mother's birthday, and I was out walking my three dogs and we watched the bright flags wave from the porches. It was mild and sunny and I got a call then from Jessica Soban, Harvard Law School's dean of admissions, who had called for an interview the week before. Now when her area code lit my screen again, I almost missed the call because I had to calm my dogs even though the three of them were just sitting serenely, watching the flags. I answered and it was Jessica, and I had been admitted from the waitlist and she was looking forward to seeing me in the fall.

It was a short call because my response was that I needed to go tell my mom, and she was kind enough to let me go, and now the four of us were sprinting home on fourteen feet past all the flags and for an instant it was as though they were celebrating me even though it was not my birthday. We all made it barking through the door and I called to Mom, and went out to the backyard to jump on the trampoline we had had there since I was a child. And in the days after, I began preparing, watching law school movies, exploring corners of the Harvard website, imagining what I would learn. And so Flag Day was like the day I had decided to go join the army after Avi died, because it gave me something new to be about. And that was wonderful, because these months had been hard, because even though I was safe, my friends and my family in Israel were not, and I would think about my three siblings every day when I was playing with my dogs.

And I would not stop thinking about my family in Be'eri or my men, but now at least I had something forward, because that was behind, and I could not go back through the yellow gate into Be'eri or back to Kisufim or the yard even though I still did these in my dreams, and even though before I went to sleep at night, I would think that right now it was morning for my men where they were, stirring in the barracks, preparing to shine their shoes and stand together, and salute their flag.

And so I became happier after Flag Day, when I took a step forward toward leaving things behind. August came and I moved to school, and at orientation there was excitement and some grief, too, and year one is hard and I was thankful to have been plucked from the waitlist so I committed myself to the books. I had not read much news from Israel in the meantime, but now and then I would tune in, and drift.

It was a Friday, September 21, 2012, that I awoke in my dorm bed and decided to check the news before class, and read that a group of Egyptian militants had breached the border and ambushed the soldiers supervising the laborers working on the fence. Netanel Yahalomi, a private in the Artillery Corps, took a bullet to his head before he could put on his helmet. Netanel, whose name meant "the Lord has given," was twenty years old.

I was late before realizing it so I grabbed my backpack and hurried to Civil Procedure with Jack Goldsmith, whose lucid, authoritative lectures made his class my favorite. I sat in my assigned seat and tuned in, because Goldsmith would cold-call students and interrogate them, and did not suffer fools. I had to focus, but I thought of Netanel and looked away from Goldsmith and across the room, and I was back in Shekef with Shmuel, and we supervised the laborers and guarded the fence, and I wondered if Netanel saw any more than this in the moment before he was hit.

I looked back to Goldsmith, to search for any import in what he was saying. But there was none, and I began shedding quiet tears, because he was unintelligible and here was not where I wanted to be. I sat without pretending not to be crying, and some classmates across the room took notice, and I saw one nudge another and a few more look my way in concern. I stood up for the restroom, left my things, and fled from the room, beyond the main restroom across the hall and up to the remote one on the second floor. Inside I sealed myself in the handicapped stall, which was even larger than our armored room at Be'eri—and yet was for me alone. And as my hands slid over the lock, I wept, for Netanel, for the friends I had left in Kisufim, for myself, here in the sterile white stall where I had hidden myself, safe from all the world outside.

After some time I saw an hour had passed, and that the class I had abandoned was ending. I waited several minutes longer, to be sure no one would remain in the room when I returned. Then I went back to the empty room to collect my things, and took the rest of the day to go home to dream, reminded of the nonlinear and weaving ways of grief.

56

In that first year I discovered an interest in the international law of war and human rights. I spent the summer after in The Hague as a law clerk at the United Nations' International Criminal Tribunal for the Former Yugoslavia, with the privilege of placement in the chambers of the Tribunal's chief appeals judge and president, Theodor Meron.

In the wake of Israel's dramatic victory in the Six-Day War in 1967, Prime Minister Levi Eshkol requested a legal opinion from his Foreign Ministry's young counsel, Theodor Meron. Did the law permit the settlement of Israeli civilians in the newly administered West Bank territories? No, wrote Meron, without equivocation. Although Israel could establish temporary military camps there, civilian settlement would violate the Fourth Geneva Convention, Article 49, paragraph 6: "The Occupying Power shall not deport or transfer parts of its own civilian population into the territory it occupies."

When I arrived at the Tribunal, the junior officer who greeted me explained that this legal titan had selected my application because he was intrigued by my CV, the one setting forth my academic history, marksmanship credentials, and West Bank deployment. Once we were past the metal detectors and within the compound, the officer advised me that the judge had set aside some time the next day to meet me in his private office.

In the morning I put on my best, stiffest suit and necktie, tightened my helmet, and got on my bike at my apartment to begin the longer of the two routes, the one headed there.

Absurd, I remember thinking as I pedaled, that there are so many bicyclists here in Holland and yet none protect themselves with helmets.

As it happened, the judge was delayed until the afternoon, which left me rather uncertainly working through the morning on the footnotes of his forthcoming appellate decision. Then the hour came, and I had twice buttoned up before I entered to face him from across the long desk in his office.

After he had inquired on events at the law school, his own alma mater, he cut to other things that bound us. He asked whether my time in the territories was connected to my interest in the international legal project. I affirmed that it was what had given birth to it.

It made sense, he said across the long desk, and he went on to talk about the broader work of the Tribunal. Law among nations, not just within them, was an essential project, he insisted. Law was our great tool to protect against our capacity to rationalize injustice. A capacity history has shown to be even more durable in nations, than it is in individuals.

I was silent, admitting this, when he added, "Your experience in the territories will help you. I have found that, for the best advocates, the work is always deeply personal," in a striking echo of what Ziv had told us, offhand, in the desert over two years prior.

Then I felt pulled to say, now that the door was opened: "Nineteen sixty-seven was almost fifty years ago, and you chose to tell the prime minister the true answer instead of the one he asked for."

He waved it off, returning to the point he had been making: the project to which this office was devoted. "Remember the importance of commitment to the project," said the eighty-three-year-old Meron, before releasing me until the morning.

In Holland, summer nights are a wonder, with a stillness,

a greenness, and reserves of quiet energy that stay bright impossibly late into the evening. The very late sundown blesses not only those later evening hours but the early ones, giving them a lovely sense of openness and promise, and it being not even five o'clock at my dismissal, I exited the compound and took pleasure in the steady click-clack of my leather soles on the pavement. I waved to the attendant at the metal detector, then unchained my bicycle, stashed my helmet in my backpack, and pedaled on the wide red lane into the warm summer evening.

57

And it felt the closest I had ever been to flying. I was not airborne, but still this was closer to flight because I was not falling either. My two knees were brought together, body parallel to the earth below, arms spread wide. I was only a leg's length above the ground, but I would stay here awhile without fear of it, and I allowed myself to close my eyes. From below came a chuckle from Ziv, my other sergeant, who was not for the first time leading me through my baby steps in a new game.

It was June 2014 in San Francisco, and on Shabbat, Ziv and I had stopped in Washington Square Park in North Beach, and set up there with coffee on the grass, choosing sun over the shade. He had let me buy his coffee, an act of immense generosity on his part, and let me host him at my apartment across town, which was the same. Because only he could do these things, and not me, and it was now two and a half years after my release, but still only he could ever be the one to do these. And along our walk, he shared with me another natural law: "V'yakum hamalafafon v'yakeh et haganan," which means, "And the cucumber will rise and strike the gardener." This was not his own law but a popular Israeli one, and I thought I knew what it meant but still did not think it was the whole truth, because I was sure the gardener had chosen to allow it—and Ziv's grin suggested this, too.

I was here for the summer with a law firm, I had told him during the walk from my Civic Center apartment toward North Beach. And we had stopped at the farmer's market on the way, and bought ripe strawberries to eat together on the bench while we watched the people. It was the summer after my second year of school, I explained, and I had taken a summer associate position at a firm here called Covington and Burling. And if all went well, I would return after graduating to begin as a full-time corporate attorney. But I was not happy at the firm, I confessed. We munched on the berries and a dribble of red juice started down my chin, and I wiped it off clean and missed a time I would not have pretended to care.

He asked if I knew the reason I was unhappy and I said there were at least a few. I told him the partners at the firm seemed colorless and flaccid, and that I dreaded a slow transformation from a summer associate on his forced best behavior into a partner on the only behavior left known to him. I told him I imagined this transformation would be painful, until it was horrifyingly not. I told him when I walked from my apartment toward the gray tower, I would pass through the Tenderloin district, past some poorer blocks where men in T-shirts watched while I clacked past in my uniform, and it was difficult to look back. I was simply not fooling myself by walking straight toward—instead of running. I told him the work was dry and the clients, too, and that these were surely not clients who needed to get any richer, but I clarified I was sure those last parts were not the worst ones.

And Ziv sat and listened, and we had finished the berries now, and he had a bit of juice on his chin and said it was obvious to him this was not the place for me, and that he hoped it was obvious to me, too. I looked at the juice on his chin and was glad he was being this honest with me, because it had been easy to say all the reasons I wanted to leave, but harder to say I would. He was right, so I thanked him, and we got going again on our walk.

I felt lighter already, because this was the first day I had made up my mind about the firm. And I listened to Ziv with love, and he began telling me of where he had been, too. He had taken the summer off and was passing through San Francisco in no hurry, and was glad I was able to put him up because he did not want to chase after money just to spend it on a hotel. In August he would be going to Burning Man, which had been a dream for years now, but one he had needed to bury while in the army, like many things. After his release he had taken up woodworking, and he loved the combination of working with his hands and heart to create things of both usefulness and beauty, and hoped to open a studio back in Israel after he returned. He had also picked up Acroyoga, a playful form of yoga for two or more, in which one lies on the ground and supports the other in the air, in a variety of free movements and positions. He found Acroyoga beautifully liberative, when he was the one in the air, the "flyer," but even more so when he was the "base," the one on the earth who watches the other fly.

And after we sat down in the park and our coffee kicked in, he proposed teaching me some simple Acroyoga. I had not done it before but loved the idea, because it was even better than hosting him or buying him coffee. So we began, and he had me base first while he flew. I lay back flat on the grass and hoisted him in the air with my legs, my toes planted at the insides of his hips as he straightened himself, his two arms straight out to the sides ready to fly. Once the base and flyer have reached equilibrium, a special thing happens, because there is no exertion for the base and no imbalance for the flyer, and they can stay where they are for about as long as they want. It took some time to get there because this was my first try, but we found it, and stayed.

Eventually we switched roles, and he let me fly in return. We reached equilibrium faster this time, and his toes on my hips were in just the right place. I opened my arms and closed my eyes, which was when that chuckle came from below, and then a question. We had been speaking mostly English, because

Ziv's was very good and my Hebrew less sharp than before. But he said some things in Hebrew when it mattered, when it was the better way to say what he wanted.

"*Hamatzav noach l'cha?*" He was asking if the position was comfortable to me, but *noach* meant not just comfortable but restful, too. And *noach* has another meaning in the army, where it refers to the "at ease" posture for a soldier, which his commander has told him he is free to assume.

I listened for the end of his question and answered in Hebrew with the words that arose: "Yes, this is great. This is just how I always thought it would be."

58.

But it was just like before. Worse. July 2014 saw the border in flames, rockets falling by the hundreds and my men being summoned for emergency reserves. This urgent summons is termed *Tzav Shmoneh*, "Order Eight," as if to count seven from *Tzav Rishon*, the first, and then begin anew after the seventh, the one of rest. So foretold the Book of Uri: *L'kol Shabbat, yesh Motzei Shabbat.* The revealed truth that running from—once one has come awake to it—is a terminal pursuit.

"Yesterday I was in the field for the alarm," Dotan relayed through the stuttering webcam.

Which field, I thought. Were you alone. Were you running in the field, blond braids in the sun, shadows nearing and the final call.

"And then we got to the *merchav mugan*," she said, and I exhaled. She had made it to the armored room. Two years had passed, but I hoped the Scotch tape still held her paper drawings to the wall, and that her humming was the loudest sound.

"*Hakol b'seder* (Is everything okay)?" she asked, as on the day we met, because I must again have drifted.

"Yes," I said. "It is good to know that, thank you."

Then the camera cut, and I returned myself to Washington Square, where the sun was bright and I could lie together with the ants speeding through the cracks in the open field.

59

Heaven had not felt closer than here, at Balos Beach on the island of Crete. We were here on business so it was not the time to get carried away, and I had not expected to pack a briefcase for my first trip to the Greek islands, but on my postgrad fellowship in Belgium, we were called for a conference at the NATO base here at Souda Bay. My supervisor, Steve, had shown me the nearby town of Chania, where we stayed, and in the evenings we walked along the harbor where the ruins of an old fortress overlooked the water, a remnant of Crete's Venetian occupation. Now a Greek flag flew from the highest point of the ruins, and the harbor lights looked up on it from below to cast its blues and whites in gold.

On the day after the conference we set our alarms early and took off in a rented car, Steve and his boyfriend Josh and I, west from Chania till the highway ended, because Balos could be reached only after leaving your tires behind. The three of us took the hike, thirty minutes down the mountain to the strip of white sand between turquoise oceans, a strip which would vary in size based only on the tide, because the grateful sand had long ago let down its last guard.

I came in from the water and sat down dripping, and bit into some of the watermelon Steve had prepacked in neat slices in the cooler. And I wiggled my toes because I heard music, a familiar rhythm, Mizrachit music playing at a polite volume from the next towels over. It had been a while since I last heard Mizrachit, flavorful Israeli music that would play at impolite volumes outside the barracks. And though this music was not for us, surely it was not too much to ask to permit myself to enjoy it while we waited, so I wiggled my toes.

My eye was drawn to my right big toe, which was covered in sand and did not want to be anywhere else. This was the toe that had absorbed the whole force of the ammunition shelf in basic training's first week, and had not forgotten the feeling. The toenail still grew, but split from the bed halfway up from the root, and past that point the nail was detached from the pink nail bed, growing out above it in a dead gray. Beneath, the soft nail bed was no longer shielded and had grown thick, as it had to. This disfigurement aside, I had exited my service free of all impairment, though the nail would look back at me, half-pink and half-dead as often as I cut my nails, which was just enough.

I turned to the source of the sound and found four Israelis hacking into the whole watermelon they had brought. They were far enough that I could look elsewhere easily, but close enough I could call to them easily, too.

"*Ma ha'inyanim, chevrei* (What's going on, guys)?" They were taken aback, but not long enough to forget their graces.

"All's good, brother. You want some watermelon?" One held a bloody dripping chunk out in the air toward me.

"I have some, but thank you." I pointed to the cooler with the neat slices arranged inside.

They understood, and then another asked how I spoke so well. I spoke with an accent, yet had already betrayed that my Hebrew did not come from a classroom. I replied that I had served in the Nachal Infantry Brigade's 50th Battalion, *Chamishim*. The four of them softened and one called back that he had served in *Chamishim*, and now he and I were *achim* (brothers) more than ever. And my brother and I sat and talked, at this distance close enough to make conversation easy, but far enough there was no mistaking our towels were different islands in the sand.

And before long, things had changed for my toe, which until now had not wanted to be anywhere else. We talked mostly of *Chamishim*, even though he had also been released long ago, because although I might have had little else in common with him, I had more in common with him than with anyone else on the archipelago. After a while he went to join his friends in the water, and the tide had lowered so I watched him sprint out to it free under the sun, then reclined faceup on my towel like Steve and Josh, who were napping on theirs. When I awoke, they had their sandals on and we would get ready to go soon, and the other four were back on their island with the music still going, and had brought out a second watermelon to hack apart.

I began to change my mind about the watermelon because I felt I would have loved a chunk quite a lot, but I also felt it was too late to ask. And when the three of us took our towels and got up to leave, I called to the other four *"Ta'asu chayim,"* which translates as "Do life," but simply means have a great time. And my brother called back, *"Shmor al atz'm'cha, achi* (Guard over yourself, brother, meaning "Take care"),* and they all four waved, and their music stayed in my ears even after we turned to leave them behind, and started heading back up the mountain to make our way home.

60.

I was home for Thanksgiving 2018 with my family in Santa Barbara, an easy drive up the Pacific Coast Highway from my rent-controlled Santa Monica apartment. This year I had been some months without steady income, since leaving another firm where I had stayed longer than I could have justified to Ziv, had he asked me. My student debt was growing daily and dreaming big, and I had yanked back my Roth IRA deposit to cover groceries, when I was reminded, Thanksgiving afternoon, that I had a few months of rent money waiting for me in Israel.

It was the soldier's final gift, for those soldiers finding themselves on the preferred side of the gift flowchart. He receives two cash disbursements: one immediately upon release and a second after five years have passed. The first, his *ma'anak shichrur* ("release grant"), is intended to aid his reentry to civilian life, and looks forward. The second, his *pikadon* ("deposit"), is intended as a tribute for his service, and looks back.

He must wait five years for the *pikadon*, but must claim it before seven or else forfeit it. I had forgotten mine, and we were playing bocce in the backyard, and I watched the pallino, which is the companionless white ball tossed to the ground for the purpose of lying still and being struck by the others. My brother David, the sharpest shot among us, delivered an exquisite throw for the other team, his red ball striking the pallino and coming to rest beside it. And I lit up, because I had just rediscovered my *pikadon* like a twenty in a pair of jeans gone through enough washes to erase Jackson's memory. Then I remembered the seven-year rule, thinking back to my release date at the end of

December 2011. I took a moment for the math, and after my team lost the game to David's, I went inside to book a flight for December.

Back in Santa Monica, I packed my discharge papers and dog tag, which were the only forms of ID I had left, and wrote to my family at Be'eri that I was coming for Chanukah. When the plane landed at Ben Gurion, it was Chanukah in the terminal already, and the *sufganiot* (Chanukah jelly donuts) were out in force, laid out on baker's sheets in hard ranks and files like the border patrol. At customs I took my tourist's stamp, the first in the empty passport I had just renewed, then bought a few *sufganiot* and sat with them on a bench in the arrivals hall, because I had a week and no mission, except to be rewarded for my mission from before.

After I had finished eating and sat long enough to make the point that I was not in a hurry, I went to the train platform, where the signs ran side by side in Hebrew and English, and I blocked out the English side and made myself work through the other. Then I was at the Tel Aviv central bus station, where I would get shawarma with my soldier's discount on the way home to Be'eri, and I decided to take the long walk to my Airbnb near the ocean. It was a warm evening, and when I got to Allenby Street and the air had grown salty, I found another bench and sat awhile to breathe it in, and to collect myself under the lights.

In the morning I walked up Ben Yehuda Street to the nearest branch of Bank Hapoalim. The army contracts with Hapoalim and Leumi, two national banks, for them to disburse the *pikadon* on its behalf, so I chose Hapoalim, where I'd had an account as a soldier. When I made it to the front of the line and the teller greeted me in English, I responded in Hebrew that I had been a soldier released some time ago and hoped to claim my *pikadon*. I slid her my discharge papers and dog tag, and she picked up the papers but left the dog tag limp on the counter, explaining that it did not help her because anyone can order a custom one on the internet for thirty shekels. I dug in my bag for my passport, regretted not bringing my expired one, which had holes punched through it and my visa from before, but I had not kept it so I slid her the clean one and she opened it to look.

She asked for my *mispar ishi* and I recited it as I had in basic, the seven-digit Hebrew name whose English translation I had never learned. She typed in the digits, then said I would need to open an account in order to receive the payment.

"Is that army policy or bank policy?" I reverted to English now, to be sure of things.

"Bank policy." She had very crisp English. "We can't write a check without the account verification process. Would you like to go ahead and open a foreigner's account?"

"Can it be opened today?"

"No, it will take about three weeks to become active."

About three weeks was the end of December, longer life than my *pikadon* had left.

"No. Not now, thank you."

I took back the three IDs I had put on the counter and went outside to Ben Yehuda, where the sun was out and it was warmer than before. I realized I was not far from the hummus restaurant that was my favorite when I would visit the city from Be'eri wearing *aleph*, so I retraced the way and was delighted to find it still open. I ordered my favorite hummus ful with heavenly brown pita, and sat out front where the people walked by, their words rising warm and organic in my belly, Hebrew like I had not heard in a while. The sun was perfect now and the hummus sublime, and with the music from the windows of the passing cars, I did not want to be anywhere else. I ate my leavened bread so grateful my *pikadon* had brought me back, even if I would not receive it. *Dayenu*, it would have been enough.

But I would try again, remembering the teller had said the account requirement was bank policy, not army policy, so I decided to check Bank Leumi. The next day I left my dog tag at the Airbnb and entered the Leumi branch and, while waiting in line, made peace with the thought of being turned away here, too. Once at the front, I slid my discharge papers and passport to the teller, and recited my seven-digit name as I had done the times before. Without further ceremony, she printed me a crisp check.

She paused after looking at it. "The amount seems small. Usually they calculate more for service in a combat role. Should I check with my director if the amount was right?"

"No thank you." I did not want anything checked with her director. "My term was short, I was a volunteer."

She nodded. "Thank you for your service."

I thanked her for thanking me, and stuffed her final gift into my bag, the last discharge of anyone's obligation, then walked outside to become one of the people on the street.

On Friday I headed to the bus station, to take the old rural bus route that would bring me back to the Negev. The next bus had not yet pulled in, and the soldiers waited in tired clusters on the curbs and walls, then rose when the bus appeared. I sized up the group by habit, saw there was room for us all, and the soldiers knew, too, placid as they filtered on. When my turn came, I stood in the doorway and counted out coins for my fare while the soldiers waited behind holding their IDs. I found the last shekel I needed and dropped it in the hand of the driver, who thanked me in practiced English. I walked to the back to leave the front seats open for the soldiers behind, took a window seat, and put on headphones as we got moving.

More soldiers boarded at the next stop and I kept my attention focused out the window while my music played, before a nudge came to my thigh as a hard black barrel arrived in the seat beside me. I turned my neck to the soldier, who was tired, and he closed his eyes and let his head rest, though he kept it straight against the seat and away from my shoulder, considering my space as he did it. The bright green beret on his epaulet told me he was in the Nachal Infantry Brigade, and I would have said to him I once was also, but he was resting now so I looked away. Despite the space he gave me, his barrel's edge had come to sit on my bare thigh below my shorts, and I snuck a look at it, a Micro Tavor, the advanced Israeli rifle that had replaced the American M4 after my time, a foreign object with which I had no fluency. I let its weight rest on my thigh while he slept, my headphones on and eyes out the window in the hills as we rode past them.

He slept awhile as we rode south, and I got off first, at the rural stop I had coordinated with Noga. I found them waiting there with the car engine idling, and they called and waved, and then we were on our way back to the yellow gate. The sun was orange behind us like I remembered, and I was glad we would make it to Be'eri while it was still light. During the drive I asked to be reminded where everyone was in school, and by the time we were at the gate, I was caught up on ages, grades, and how far away the army was. Paz was seventeen and would enter conscription the following summer. Arad was fifteen, and he and his friends would soon start mulling the question of whether to aim for combat service, a decision Izzy had promised he would let Arad make when it was time. Dotan was still several years out from conscription so she spoke of school instead, but by now her long blond braids had given way to straight combed hair.

Noga and Izzy held the same jobs at the laundry center

and petting zoo, but the family had been reassigned to a new house in accord with the needs of the community, and this new one we entered was larger and beautiful inside, but farther from the yellow gate. Inside, our dinner table was already set, with places also for Noga's mother and father, who would be coming from their house soon to join. Izzy headed to the *cheder ochel* to pick up food to bring home for dinner, and the rest of us stayed in the kitchen and ate oranges from the orchards, which were now in season. When Noga's parents arrived, we lit the menorah together, and then Izzy returned with stacks of hot food and asked if I was ready for some *chamim v'taim*.

After we'd finished eating, I went out for a walk, and Izzy offered to join. As we came to the main road, he suggested going to the exhibition hall, where there was an event tonight, and on the way began to explain what it was for. In 2018, Hamas had commenced a new method of attack: instead of deadly rockets, kites and balloons. Set aflame and launched into Israel to light its fields in red and burn them to black. These toys did not travel with a rocket's speed or strike with its force; did not trigger *Tzeva Adom* because they were not weapons of war but symbols of childhood burning in effigy. Even though they were not forewarned by three calls and proclaimed by a fourth, if you were in the field and a kite came screaming, you would have time to escape. It would not kill you, because it was fired by a hunter who now dispensed with all pretense that his aim was to do that.

Izzy explained these were known as "terror kites" and "terror balloons," names that were plain and probably best. It felt like a war on the earth itself, because when rockets hit the land, they caused damage that could be repaired, but the new weapons had taken vast expanses of farmland and nature trails, all the colors of their grass and flowers, and brought them to the same shade of dead.

As we passed Dotan's playground and shelter, I remembered the bright balloons my mother would inflate for my birthday when I was a boy, and the *kalaniot* that would have carpeted the hills a couple months from now. I had not spoken as Izzy went on, and as we neared the hall, he explained that Be'eri was displaying art created by residents of the area in response to the trauma of the season. Tonight at the hall was a gathering for the artists, and for others to meet them and share in their stories. As we entered, a guitarist stood onstage playing solo and singing to an audience in rows before him, and while I listened, I walked along the walls, among the sculptures, paintings, photographs by artists on the summer they had lived together.

The first was a painting of a flaming field, no humans but the earth alive and crying, trees turned to the sky, branches as arms outstretched to heaven asking why. Beneath the earth's surface, a mother mouse and her boy hiding, his eyes shut, his mother cradling him and looking upward as the flames soared. Her eyes led above to a panicked dove, wings racing to escape from the surface.

Next was a ceramic sculpture of a stalk of wheat. One side of the stalk thick and full for harvest, the other lifeless, charred to the core. A farmer, I imagined, though I did not check the name of the artist on this piece or the one before.

Then a photograph of an open field after the flames had passed over, leaving only blackened earth. But there was another thing left behind: at the center were colors amid the black. A girl in a bright dress stood alone and looked away, gaze not down to her feet nor to the sky but straight to the horizon, toward only more dead earth. I was gripped by the colors of her dress and her braids resting on it, and watched her in the image as the artist sang. She must have been only several years old, and her long blond braids made her look just like little Dotan, who turned to face me, braids whirling, blue eyes resting on me like the day she showed me the shelter, waiting, and my eyes shook themselves and stared again into the field, and the singer's voice returned to my ears and the faceless girl had turned. She stood fixed, stared away from me into the black horizon, braids aglow as golden embers in the ashes around her.

We stayed late in the hall, because Izzy had many friends there to talk to and I did not feel rushed to leave. I did not know anyone besides him so I stayed along the walls, watching the images of trauma lining the edges of the room and Izzy and his friends laughing in the center. *A man needs to laugh and cry with the same eyes*, I remembered from an Amichai poem Eli once read me in his own loving translation. *A man doesn't have time*. Then the laughing wound down as the lights dimmed, so Izzy came to find me and we walked outside. I admitted I had known nothing of the terror kites and balloons, because I was no longer following the news like I used to. He said he did not see it as news, and I agreed without saying more, and we kept walking back past the quiet houses toward theirs, where the others slept. There, in the window of the *cheder ochel*, was a magnificent menorah burning oil for the sixth night. It had not been alight on our walk over to the hall, which meant they had lit its flames after nightfall, after the entry of Shabbat. Against the Sabbath law. At Be'eri nobody speaks the tongue of angels, I smiled to myself, as Izzy long ago had taught.

The next day was Shabbat, and I slept late. Noga had more fruit and cake set out for breakfast and I sat to eat with the others. I asked about the swimming pool but they reminded me it was closed for winter, so instead we drove for a hike in the afternoon, and on the way home stopped at the orchards to pick more oranges. We came back with whole bags of them, and Noga was already setting up for the *al-ha-aish* we would have that evening, for my last night at Be'eri before I flew home on *Yom Rishon*.

But while it was still light, I sneaked away for a visit to my field. I arrived there and found myself alone in late afternoon as I loved, and sat on the hillside. I looked down at the earth below, and did not stand up to start running, to sail freely over the field as in my dream. I did not need to try to fly over the earth to know my feet would plod heavy over it instead, eyes raked by the sun, lungs heaving firsts without seconds. So I looked on from above the field without stepping down onto it, and guarded what was true from what was dreamed.

I knew that back at the house Dotan and the others waited and maybe wondered where I was, but I did not think they knew where to find me. I sat on the hill free of that worry, and watched the swaying orange trees, eyes open even as the sun dipped beyond the barbed wire, filling them with light. After it had kissed the horizon and the sky began to turn, I came to feel it was time to get up to go, while the sun still shone on me at the top of the hill, and before its last golden rays slipped away from the field below, where the ripened oranges lay on the hard earth.

ABOUT THE AUTHOR

Ben Bastomski, a Southern California native and Israel Defense Forces veteran, moved to Santa Monica, CA to practice law after graduating from Harvard Law School in 2015. In the years since, Ben has become an accomplished civil litigator, while pursuing a parallel career as a fashion model with a Los Angeles talent agency. He has recently returned to live in Israel. Ben was raised in a Jewish home with a love of furry and feathered animals, creation myths, and the outdoors. Among his most beloved childhood memories were the signings he attended at his favorite local bookstore, Chaucer's Books. *As Figs in Autumn* is his début book.